The Story Of The Old World

Henry William Elson

In the interest of creating a more extensive selection of rare historical book reprints, we have chosen to reproduce this title even though it may possibly have occasional imperfections such as missing and blurred pages, missing text, poor pictures, markings, dark backgrounds and other reproduction issues beyond our control. Because this work is culturally important, we have made it available as a part of our commitment to protecting, preserving and promoting the world's literature. Thank you for your understanding.

Foundation History Series

THE STORY OF THE OLD WORLD

BY

HENRY W. ELSON, Ph.D., Litt.D.
PROFESSOR OF HISTORY AND POLITICAL SCIENCE, OHIO UNIVERSITY
Author of "History of the United States," "Side Lights on American History," etc.

AND

CORNELIA E. MacMULLAN, Ph.D.
HEAD OF DEPARTMENT OF ENGLISH, MONTCLAIR STATE NORMAL SCHOOL

YONKERS-ON-HUDSON : : : NEW YORK
WORLD BOOK COMPANY
1915

FOUNDATION HISTORY SERIES

By Henry W. Elson *and*
Cornelia E. MacMullan

THE STORY OF OUR COUNTRY: Book I
Cloth. viii + 216 pages. Illustrated. Four colored maps. *From the period of discovery to the end of the Revolutionary War.*

THE STORY OF OUR COUNTRY: Book II
Cloth. viii + 283 pages. Illustrated. Four colored maps. *From the end of the Revolutionary War to the election of President Wilson.*

THE STORY OF THE OLD WORLD
Cloth. viii + 248 pages. Illustrated. Seven colored maps. *An account of those periods or events in European history that have direct and easily traceable bearing upon the development of the American republic.*

COPYRIGHT, 1911, BY WORLD BOOK COMPANY

EMSOW-2

From the Painting by Woodville

ALFRED, CHOSEN KING BY HIS WARRIORS

PREFACE

ALL of Old-World history is the New World's heritage; no historian would assert in regard to the most remote and seemingly insignificant occurrence of ancient record that it had no influence upon the course of later human events. But there are certain events connected with earlier human progress that have had a direct and easily traceable influence upon our New-World destinies; a knowledge of these is essential to a full understanding and enjoyment of the story of our country.

A committee of eight eminent teachers, reporting upon the study of American history in our schools, has declared that too much emphasis is placed upon the Atlantic Ocean as a barrier between the history of the New World and that of the Old. This book is written to meet that criticism. It is not a condensed "general history." It is, in reality, the story of our country carried beyond and behind that wall habitually erected by earlier school historians upon the borders of the Atlantic.

CONTENTS

CHAPTER I

AMERICANS 1
    Immigrants (1). — The coming of the Germans (5). — When America was unknown (11). — Useful inventions (13).

CHAPTER II

THE GREEKS 17
    The Siege of Troy (21). — The Battle of Marathon (27). — Leonidas and the Three Hundred (31). — Salamis (34). — The city wall (35). — Pericles and Athens (38). — The Greek boy (42). — The Olympic games (46).

CHAPTER III

RULERS OF GREECE 49
    The government of Athens (49). — Solon (51). — The Story of Socrates (54). — The boyhood of Alexander the Great (58). — The Conquests of Alexander (61).

CHAPTER IV

ROME AND THE ROMANS 67
    The City of the Seven Hills (67). — Horatius at the Bridge (69). — The Sacred Mount (72). — Cincinnatus (74). — The first Punic War and Regulus (76). — The second Punic War and Hannibal (78). — Cornelia's jewels (82).

CHAPTER V

CÆSAR AND THE WEST 87
    Early life of Cæsar (87). — Two great Romans (89). — Cæsar and the Gauls (91). — The Story of Vercingetorix (95). — Crossing the Rubicon (98). — Last Years and Death of Cæsar (101). — The Empire and the City (103). — The Coming of Christianity (107). — What Rome gave to the World (112).

CONTENTS

CHAPTER VI

HEIRS TO THE ROMANS 115

    The Story of Clovis (116). — The Story of King Arthur (118). — The Vikings (121). — Alfred becomes King (123). — The Greatest of the English Kings (126). — Beginnings of American Liberty (130). — The English Parliament (135). — The Welsh and the Scots (138). — The Manor of the Middle Ages (139). — The Walled Town (142). — Training for Knighthood (144). — The Canterbury Cathedral (146).

CHAPTER VII

THE CRUSADES 148

    The First Crusade (149). — King Richard and the Third Crusade (154). — The Results of the Crusades (159).

CHAPTER VIII

THE WESTERN WORLD 165

    The Northmen (165). — Marco Polo (168). — The Voyage of Diaz (170). — Christopher Columbus (172). — The Name America (177). — John Cabot (178). — Vasco da Gama (180). — Balboa and the South Sea (182). — Magellan's Voyage (184). — Jacques Cartier (187). — Cortez and Mexico (191). — The Search for Gold (195).

CHAPTER IX

EUROPEAN CLAIMS TO AMERICA 200

    Sir Francis Drake (202). — The Gentle Lord de Bayard (206). — The Fate of Fort Carolina (208). — Spain and the Dutch (211). — William of Orange (213). — The Story of Sir Philip Sidney (216). — The Invincible Armada (217). — The Story of Gilbert and Raleigh (220).

SUGGESTIVE TOPICS FOR COMPOSITION AND DISCUSSION . . 225

BIBLIOGRAPHY 233

THE STORY OF THE OLD WORLD

CHAPTER I

AMERICANS

IN almost every city or community in the United States there are families who came from foreign lands. Some of them have been in this country a long time and perhaps the children were born here; others came more recently and children as well as parents were born abroad.

In some parts of the country a very large proportion of the people are newcomers. In Minnesota and other states lying near it a great many of the people are Scan′di-na′vi-ans — Swedes, Nor-we′gi-ans, or Danes — or, rather, they were until recently. Now they are Americans. They came to America to make it their permanent home. They purchased or rented small farms and went to work to make a living. They are industrious, good people. Some of them have risen to high positions. Not long ago an American-born Swede was governor of Minnesota and others have served in the United States Senate.

If now we go back a hundred years or more we shall find that the ancestors of all of us came from foreign lands — from the same countries that we see on the map of Europe. We are all Eu′ro-pe′ans a few generations back. We are a transplanted people. And the Europeans are still coming, in great numbers.

Nearly three hundred years ago, when Massachusetts was being settled, about twenty thousand people came to that colony in the space of ten years — from 1630 to 1640 — an average of two thousand a year. This was called the "Great Migration." What would our ancestors have thought could they have foreseen the present human river flowing to our shores from Europe — more than a million a year?

An emigrant ship of 1630

If we could spend a day at Ellis Island, near New York City, where most of the immigrants land, we should probably see thousands of these people debark from the incoming ships. In colonial days they came in small sailing vessels and two or three months were spent on the sea. Now they come in great, swift steamships, often called "ocean greyhounds," and seldom are they more than a week on the ocean.

An ocean greyhound

The immigrants on landing are all examined by inspectors. Each must pay a small fee for the privilege of remaining. If one is a criminal, or diseased,

The old-world mother of America

or likely to become a pauper, he is sent back. After the immigrants have passed the test of our immigration

In a New Land
By permission of Century Co.

laws, they begin the task of earning a living. Some go to the far West, others to the South, but many remain in the large cities of the East. Those who go far into the interior of the continent have another long and toilsome journey ahead of them before they reach their future homes. Most railroads have special immigrant cars, with hard, cushionless seats, on which a lower fare is charged, and into these cars the people are crowded for their journey to other parts of the country.

Why do these people come here? Look at them as they arrive and most of them seem very poor. Their clothing is coarse and their goods are tied up in rough bundles. Many of them cannot speak the English language. It is true there may be a criminal or anarchist among them; but the great majority of them are good people, honest and industrious, and they come to America in the hope of doing better for themselves and for their children than they could do in the Old World. They have done a brave deed in leaving the home of their childhood and crossing the great ocean to better their condition. A lazy, shiftless person would not do such a thing. In a few years the children learn our language, and often the parents too. In time they will learn our ways and become good Americans. The one thing above all else that makes good Americans is our public schools.

We are fond of believing that our ancestors who braved the Atlantic billows to find a home in the New World were heroes, and perhaps they were; but many of the late comers have shown the same kind of courage.

THE COMING OF THE GERMANS

Let us now go back to colonial times and take a hurried view of one of the settlements, as an example of all. Which shall we choose?

From "The Story of Our Country" you have read of the coming of the Pilgrim Fathers in the *Mayflower*. You have also read of the first settlement at Jamestown in Virginia, of the early settlement of New York by the Dutch, of the coming of William Penn to Pennsylvania and of General Oglethorpe to Georgia. These are treated in nearly all our histories. But how many know about the first settlement of the Germans?

Emigrants on Shipboard

Seldom is there much said about them in our school histories; perhaps because they were not among the first settlers and did not found a separate colony.

They are a great people and the German Empire is one of the most powerful nations of to-day. The Germans have played a great part in building up America to what it is now. It was a German, Waldsee Müller, who first suggested that the vast lands of the Western World be called America. The only man who founded two of the original thirteen colonies was a German — Peter Minuit, the founder of New York and Delaware. In both cases he led a people not of his own blood — the Dutch to New York and the Swedes to Delaware. It was a German who summoned the first Colonial Congress, in New York, in 1691 — Jacob Leisler. There was one German, named Tyrker, with Leif Ericson on his first voyage to the American shores, 1000 A.D.; there were a few Germans among the first settlers at Jamestown and a few in the still earlier settlement at Port Royal, South Carolina. Moreover, there are twenty million of the people of the United States to-day who are of German descent, through one or both parents. Only the English surpass them in this respect, and they but little. All others fall far below them. For these reasons and because the early coming of the Germans is not well known, we have chosen to give a brief narrative of their first settlement.

WILLIAM PENN

The first settlement of Germans was in Pennsylvania. You have read about William Penn and the Quakers who founded Philadelphia. Before coming to America Penn went to Germany, where he made many friends. A few years later, when he received a charter from the king of England, a number of Germans became interested and decided to go to the new land of Penn. The first shipload of Germans came from Crefeld, a city on the Rhine River. They came in the good ship *Concord*, which was to them what the *Mayflower* was to the Pilgrim Fathers. It was a strong, roomy vessel, and its commander was Captain Jeffreys.

The company of German emigrants was not a large one; there were thirteen families and a devoutly religious people they were. It was in midsummer, 1683, when they launched out upon the deep sea for the long

The Site of Philadelphia and the "Treaty Tree"

journey to their new home in the Western World. We can imagine how the tears must have filled their eyes when they saw fading from view the shores of the land they were leaving behind, the land of their childhood's home, which they never expected to see again.

After a voyage of two and a half months the *Concord* reached the mouth of the Delaware. It was in the early autumn, when the forests are dressed in rainbow colors and all nature is so charming and so inviting. How refreshing the sight of land must have been to these weary travelers after the long weeks upon their floating home, where nothing met the eye but the ceaseless rolling billows around them.

The *Concord* sailed up the Delaware and reached Philadelphia on October 6, 1683. One year before this William Penn had arrived from England and had

William Penn's House

already laid out the new city on the western bank of the Delaware. He was expecting the Germans, some of whom were Quakers, and he received them with a warm welcome.

The real leader of this German colony did not come in the *Concord;* he had arrived in another ship a few weeks earlier. His name was Daniel Pas-to'ri-us. He was a very learned man and spoke several languages. Pastorius came to be an intimate friend of William Penn and the two dined together twice a week. In later years Pastorius wrote that Philadelphia, then a village of a few houses, was surrounded by dense forests and that sometimes he lost his way in the underbrush when going to Penn's house.

The first thing to be decided when the German colonists arrived was where to make their home. Through their leader, Pastorius, and a company in Germany, they had purchased from William Penn a large tract of land, thousands of acres, for about ten cents an acre. But just where this land was to be set apart for them was not determined.

At length it was decided that they settle about six miles north of Philadelphia, and thither they went. Faithfully they toiled in cutting away the timbers, clearing the land for planting, and building homes. Pastorius wrote that his house was thirty feet long and fifteen feet broad, and that for a window glass he used oil-soaked paper. He put a Latin motto over his door, of which the English would be, "A poor home, but good cheer." When Penn first visited him at the new house he had a hearty laugh at the motto and encouraged his friend to continue building.

GERMANTOWN

The new settlement was called Germantown. It was a happy community. By the next spring streets had been laid out and patches cleared for planting. Cottages had sprung up here and there and the shouts of playing children rang out among the forest trees. Others soon came from Germany and settled at Germantown, and it became one of the most prosperous settlements in America. Many of the people were weavers and they set up looms and opened a store in Philadelphia for the sale of their wares. The town founded by Germans has long been absorbed by the great city, but that part of Philadelphia is still called by the old name — Germantown.

The people of Germantown were so busy with their farming and weaving that it was difficult to find men to hold office, and at length a fine was imposed on anyone who refused. How strange this seems to our generation; we have more office seekers than offices. The people of Germantown were sober and industrious, and criminals were so few that the courts often adjourned because they had nothing to do.

One thing more must be said about the Germans of Germantown — that by which they will be longest remembered. Negro slavery then existed in all the colonies, north and south. It was hateful to the Germans and they were the first in America to raise their voice against it. On April 18, 1688, the settlers of Germantown met and drew up a protest against slavery. This precious document is still preserved, in the handwriting of Pastorius. It was drawn up to be sent to the meeting of the Quakers, which was soon to take place. The Quakers received the protest against this traffic in human beings and acknowledged it. But they did not act upon it, and seventeen years went by before the Quakers passed resolutions against slavery. The honor of being first in the field to raise their voice against slavery in America must ever be awarded to the Pennsylvania Germans.

WHEN AMERICA WAS UNKNOWN

It seems strange that but little more than four hundred years ago half the land area of the earth was wholly unknown to the people of the other half, and that only one hundred years ago a large part of the United States was an unbroken wilderness. The land was covered with vast forests, or rolling prairies, and was inhabited only by scattered tribes of a savage race who knew nothing of civilization. How long these people, whom we call Indians, had lived here before the coming of the white man we do not know — perhaps thousands of years. The Indians had no books and no literature and had not recorded their own history. Where they came from and who they were we can only guess. All we know is that here we found them, that they could tell us nothing of their remote past, and that few of them could do more than hunt and fish.

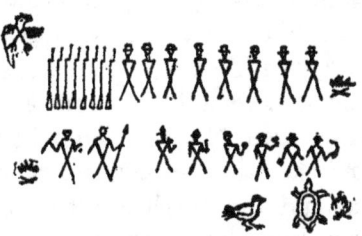

Indian Picture Writing

Fifteen hundred years before the discovery of America by white men, the Christian era began. During these intervening fifteen centuries Europe slowly advanced in civilization. The known world at the beginning of the Christian era was very small compared to the world we know. It consisted of a few countries around the Med'i-ter-ra'ne-an Sea and was under a single government — the government of Rome.

The people of Italy were then called Romans; now they are known as Italians. The inhabitants of France were called Gauls, and later Franks, while the people who lived in England were Britons. The names England and English came into use centuries later.

In those early days the people had strange notions about the earth. We know that the earth is a vast globe swinging in space around the sun, making one of its sublime revolutions every year and turning on its axis once in twenty-four hours, making the sun, moon, and stars seem to rise and set. The people did not then know these things. They believed the earth to be flat and that the sun and moon revolved around it. They thought the earth was the center of the universe and that Europe was the top and center of the earth.

There was no end to the fantastic beliefs of those days. Some thought the earth sloped downward in all directions and if a vessel sailed too far down the slope it could never get back. If the earth is round, they said, certainly nobody could live on the other side. How could they walk with their heads downward? Some believed that far to the southward the ocean was so hot that the water boiled with fury and that nothing could live in it. Another belief was that a great bird hovered over the sea, so great that it could carry off a ship in its talons.

These absurd notions were gradually dispelled as men came to study science and to know more about nature. And their study brought about a great many useful inventions, some of which we feel that we could not do without. Let us notice a few of these.

USEFUL INVENTIONS

We all know of the wonderful advantage of modern inventions. Take the telephone for example. If we wish to order something from the grocer, or speak to a friend in a distant town, or call a doctor at night, we simply go to an instrument on the wall or on our table and talk into it. Our voice is carried through a wire by means of electricity. What a marvelously strange thing this would 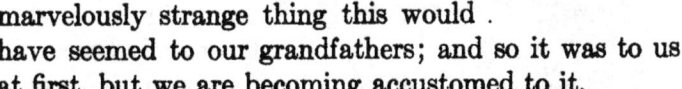 have seemed to our grandfathers; and so it was to us at first, but we are becoming accustomed to it.

Take another example — the sewing machine. Sixty or seventy years ago all sewing had to be done by hand, and a great majority of women and many men in the factories spent their time with the needle and thimble in slavish toil. The sewing machine has changed all that; it has freed women as no other invention has done. It has enabled her to give more attention to study and culture and has thus perhaps played as great a part as any other invention in raising our standard of civilization.

The past hundred years have produced more great inventions than any preceding century, but we must not think that our age has originated everything useful. If we go back to the time of Columbus and before, we shall find inventions that we could not well get along without. Among these are the mariner's compass, gunpowder, and printing.

In the ancient world all printing was done by hand. The great books of ancient times — the Bible, Homer's poems, and the like — were all preserved by hand printing. For one to reproduce a copy of the Bible in this way required several years of tedious toil.

The Manuscript
Fragment from mural painting by Alexander in Library of Congress

Books as we have them did not exist in those early times. In As-syr′i-a they wrote on clay tablets and then baked the tablets to make the writing hard and lasting. In Egypt they used papyrus, and from this we get our word "paper." The papyrus was a tall, rush-like plant, which was split and the pieces gummed together. In Asia Minor and other places they used parchment, made of the skins of goats and other animals. A fine kind of parchment, made of calfskin, was called vellum. On all these the work of printing was done by hand.

The invention of printing from movable type dates from about the middle of the fifteenth century. The inventor was John Gu′ten-berg of Mainz, a city on the Rhine river in Germany. It was about the year 1450 that Gutenberg began printing. His type was carved out of wood. The art of printing soon spread to the

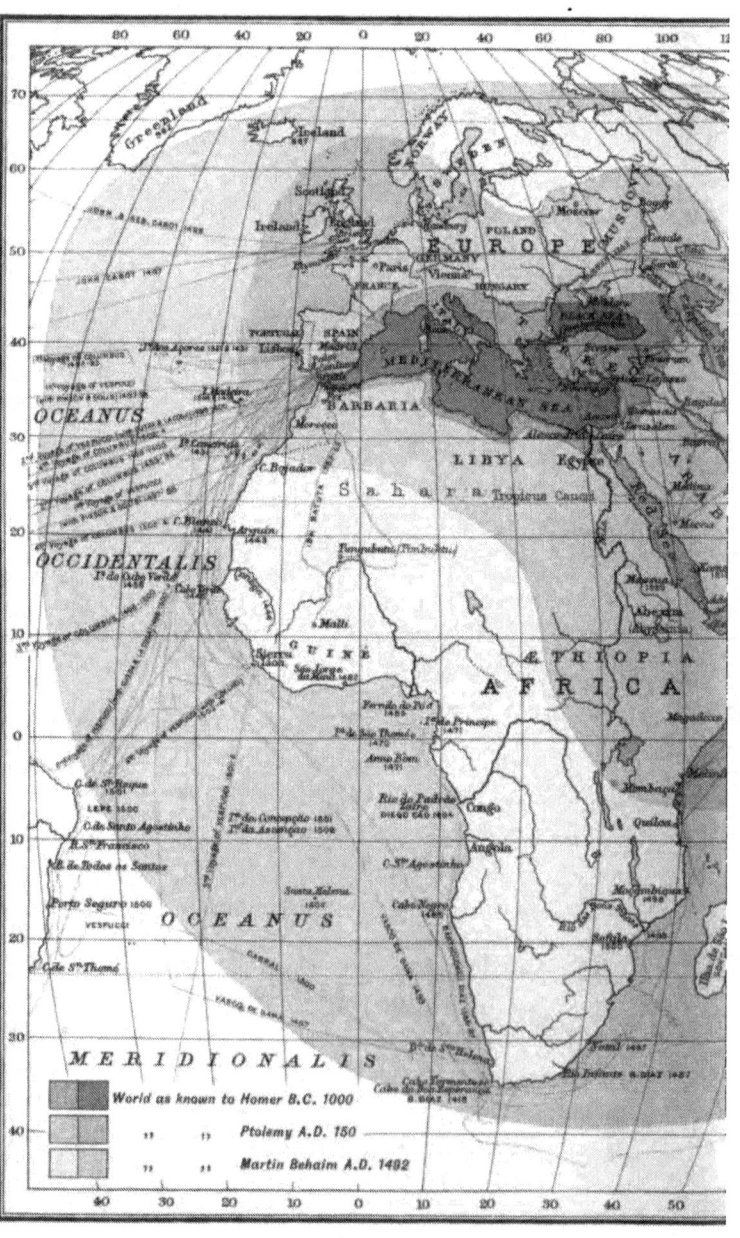

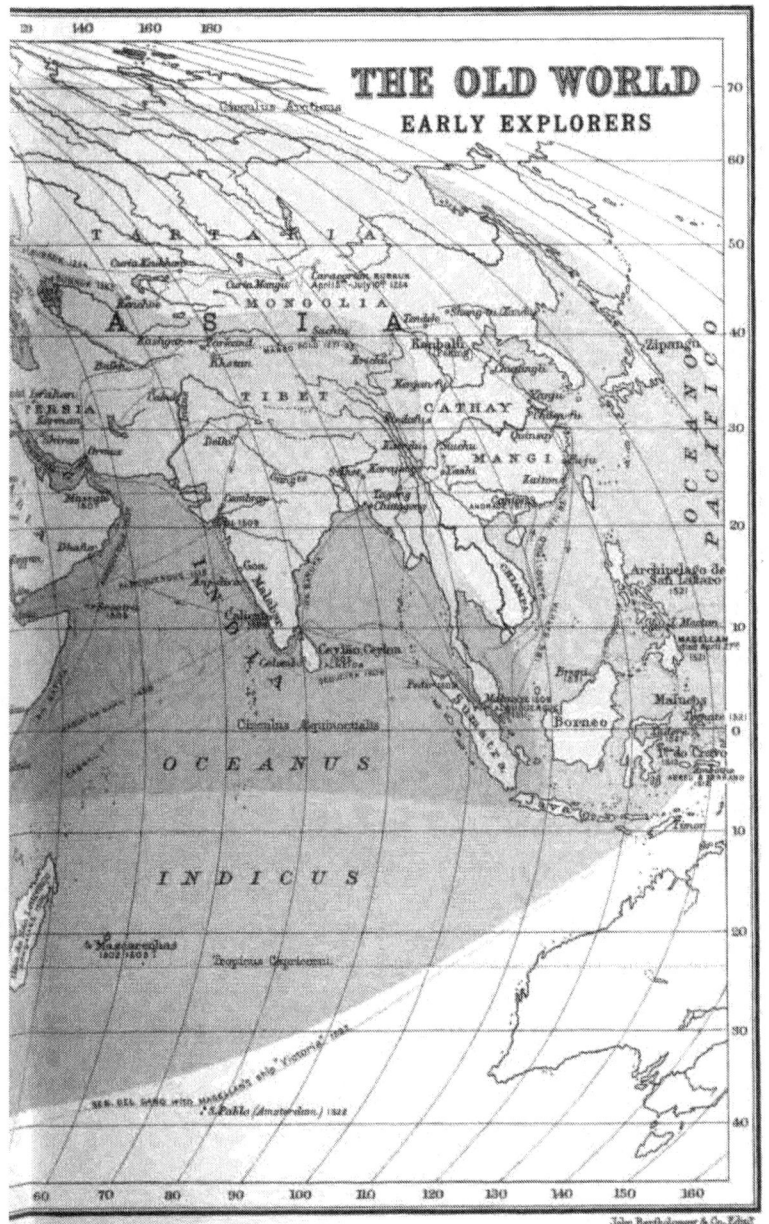

other countries of Europe. From that time to the present the art has grown and improved and to-day it constitutes one of the most extensive of modern industries. The great cylinder printing presses are among the wonders of the large cities and vast numbers of books and papers are turned out by them. When all printing was done by hand, books were few and expensive, while newspapers and magazines did not exist. It was very difficult to acquire an education in those remote days. In our own times books and papers are so cheap and so plentiful that anyone who wishes may use them.

The invention of printing naturally brings to mind another, which is very much older — the invention of the alphabet.

The American Indians used a sort of picture writing to express their thoughts.

Hieroglyphics
From a mural painting by Alexander
in Library of Congress

The ancient Egyptians used characters that we call hi'er-o-glyph'ics, and the Assyrians a wedge-shaped character which they made in soft clay and then baked. In all these the characters stood for words or objects and not for sounds, as do the letters of our alphabet.

The Phœ-ni'ci-ans, a people who lived on the eastern shore of the Mediterranean, were the inventors of the alphabet; that is, characters to represent different sounds. We do not know the exact time of the invention, but it was probably about one thousand years before Christ. From the Phœnicians the Greeks learned to write by means of letters and the Romans learned the same from the Greeks. The Romans changed the shape of many of the letters to about the form in which we now have them.

John Gutenberg
From an old print

By these few examples we see that many of the advantages we enjoy have come to us from the far past and are not of our own making. In the following chapters we shall take a closer view of the two most wonderful countries of antiquity and note some of the things they contributed to our modern life in America.

𝕻𝖔𝖘𝖙 𝖔𝖇𝖎𝖙𝖚𝖒 𝕮𝖆𝖝𝖙𝖔𝖓 𝖜𝖔𝖑𝖚𝖎𝖙 𝖙𝖊 𝖛𝖎𝖚𝖊𝖗𝖊 𝖈𝖚𝖗𝖆
𝖂𝖎𝖑𝖑𝖊𝖑𝖒𝖎. 𝕮𝖍𝖆𝖚𝖈𝖊𝖗 𝖈𝖑𝖆𝖗𝖊 𝖕𝖔𝖊𝖙𝖆 𝖙𝖚𝖎
𝕹𝖆𝖒 𝖙𝖚𝖆 𝖓𝖔𝖓 𝖘𝖔𝖑𝖚𝖒 𝖈𝖔𝖒𝖕𝖗𝖊𝖘𝖘𝖎𝖙 𝖔𝖕𝖚𝖘𝖈𝖚𝖑𝖆 𝖙
𝕳𝖆𝖘 𝖖𝖚𝖔𝖖 𝖘 𝖑𝖆𝖚𝖉𝖊𝖘.𝖓𝖚𝖘𝖘𝖎𝖙 𝖍𝖎𝖈 𝖊𝖘𝖘𝖊 𝖙𝖚𝖆𝖘

Specimen of Gutenberg's Type

CHAPTER II

The Greeks

IN ancient times, long before America was discovered by Christopher Columbus, there lived in a little country called Greece a people highly civilized and noted for their love of nature and works of art. Many of their ideas and institutions have come down to us, and we Americans, as well as other civilized nations, owe them much.

Where is Greece and who were these people? As we look on the map of Europe we find three peninsulas extending into the Mediterranean Sea. The most eastern is the Balkan, and the southern part of this peninsula is Greece.

Greece is a mountainous country with a broken coastline. Many little islands dot the seas and bays that touch its shore. The most beautiful sea that washes its shores is the blue Æ-ge'an. The islands of this sea are not only rich in minerals, but they afford an easy voyage for the navigator who crosses the waters to Asia Minor, where Greece first established her colonies.

The situation of Greece and the formation of its

land surface gave it many advantages — a varied and beautiful landscape, access to the older countries of the East, and power as an independent country. Olives, grapes, and wheat grew in the valleys and on the hill slopes. Mines of copper and silver and quarries of marble were found among the rocks. Its ranges of mountains protected it against invading forces. These ranges afforded boundaries for cantons or independent states. Wherever the Greeks settled they showed the same independence that characterized their mother country. Greece was small, but nearly every one of its states had contact with the sea, and this influenced the Greeks to colonize and thus spread their civilization.

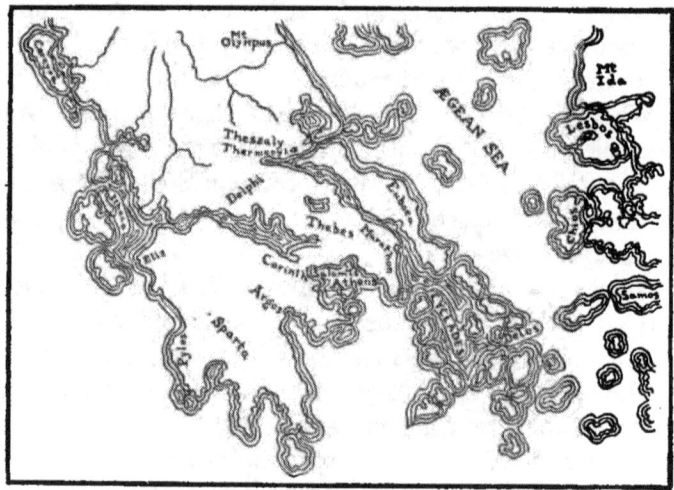

Greece and her islands

They believed the earth to be flat and that Greece occupied the middle of it. They thought that the earth was divided into halves by the Mediterranean Sea.

The Greeks enjoyed living in the outdoor air. Their theaters were left open to the sky, and many of their legislative halls and temples had no roofs. Their fondness for nature was seen in their early religion. Their gods and goddesses dwelt on the mountains and revealed themselves in the various aspects of nature. Zeus (Roman name, Jupiter) hurled the thunderbolt and scourged with lightning; Hermes (Mercury) was the personification of the wind; and Eos (Aurora) was the goddess of the dawn.

Apollo Belvidere

Since O-lym'pus was the highest and least accessible of their mountains, the ancient Greeks thought it to be the abode of their great god Zeus, the king of heaven. Here dwelt also Hera (Juno), his wife, the queen of heaven; A-the'ne (Minerva), his favorite child, the goddess of wisdom; A-pol'-lo, his son, the god of music and the god of the sun; Ar'te-mis (Diana), Apollo's sister, the goddess of the

Diana hunting with her Maidens
From the painting by Makart, in Metropolitan Museum, New York

moon and the patron of the chase. These ancient Greeks believed in many gods and goddesses. Po-sei'don (Neptune) was king of the seas, and Hades (Pluto) lord of the lower world. The goddess of love and beauty was Aph'ro-di'te (Venus). Ares (Mars) was the god of war, and his brother He-phæs'tus (Vulcan) god of fire. Hestia (Vesta) was patroness of hearth and home, and De-me'ter (Ceres) the goddess of the fruitful earth.

Redrawn from the painting by Guido Reni

Aurora

The Greek myths and legends tell of these hero gods and goddesses. One of these legends is that of the siege of Troy. The story of the Trojan War was well known to the Greeks before a poet put the legend into a poem. They regarded that war as the great event of their early history.

Of the poems that treated of the Trojan War, the "Il'i-ad" and the "Od'ys-sey" have been preserved. They are called the Ho-mer'ic poems because the

Greeks accepted them as the works of Homer, a blind poet. They give us pictures of the life of the ancient Greeks when each state was ruled by a king whose authority was supposed to descend from Zeus. The legend tells us that the descendants of Zeus founded Troy, or Il'i-um, in the northwestern part of Asia Minor, and the "Iliad" is the story of the siege of Troy.

THE SIEGE OF TROY

One of the states of ancient Greece was Sparta, and Men'e-la'us was its king. His wife was the fairest woman of her time — the beautiful Helen. She had many suitors before her marriage with Menelaus, but these wooers had agreed that they would uphold the rights of the successful suitor if it should ever become necessary. And it was not long before their help was needed.

Helen of Troy
Fragment from painting by Lord Leighton

The goddess of discord caused the trouble. At a wedding feast among the gods she threw upon the banquet table a golden apple which bore the inscription, "To the fairest." Hera, Athene, and Aphrodite quarreled for its possession. "Power has the best right to it," said Hera. "The wisdom of the gods surpasses power," replied Athene. Aphrodite smiled at what they said. "Who has greater claims than the goddess of beauty?" she asked. The quarrel grew bitter and he who was chosen as umpire was not to be envied.

The decision was referred to Paris, the son of Priam, King of Troy. A handsome and attractive young man was this judge, and each goddess tried to bias him in her favor. "Award the prize to me," said Hera, "and I will give you great wealth and unlimited power." Then Athene, in glittering armor, promised him glory and renown in war if he would give the golden apple to her. But their bribes were nothing to Paris in comparison with Aphrodite's promise, "I will give you a bride as fair as myself if you will prefer me." The handsome young judge no longer hesitated.

> "Ere yet her speech was finished, he consigned
> To her soft hand the fruit of burnished rind."

But where was Paris to find this fair bride? The answer to that lay with the goddess of beauty. She advised him to go to Greece and visit the King of Sparta, and that is what he did. The prince from Troy was graciously received by Menelaus and his beautiful queen. But he was not there many days before the king was called away from home. "Now is your opportunity," said Aphrodite. Would Paris prove false to the king who had generously entertained him? "Helen is the fairest of women and she is the bride destined for me," he said. No sooner had Men'e-la'us departed than Paris persuaded Helen to leave the court of Sparta and sail with him to Troy.

What happened when the king returned? Messengers were despatched in every direction to summon the chieftains of Greece and those suitors who had sworn to defend him. And it was not long before the Greeks were ready to embark for Troy to avenge the stealing of Helen. They accordingly set sail and soon hostilities began.

For nine years the Greeks tried to enter Troy; but they could not take the city so long as the brave Hector defended it. And in all those years the Trojans could not drive the enemy from their shores.

It was now the tenth year of the siege. A dreadful sickness had broken out among the Greeks, and many of their brave warriors had died. It seemed as if they would be forced to yield to the might of the Trojans. "If we had only A-chil'les!" they exclaimed in their despair; "the gods have truly forsaken us."

Who was Achilles and why was he not on the battlefield? He was the bravest of the Greek warriors, but Ag'a-mem'non, the brother of Menelaus, had offended him and he was now sulking in his tent.

Messenger after messenger had gone to urge the Greek warrior to return to the field, but he would not yield. Now Pa-tro'clus went, whom Achilles loved as a brother. "He certainly will not refuse him," said the Greeks. In this they were mistaken; even his friend could not persuade Achilles to return. However, he gave Patroclus his armor, and his friend took the field in the guise of Achilles. Hector was deceived, but he had no fear; he rushed upon Patroclus and slew him.

When Achilles heard that his friend was killed he

renounced his wrath and prepared to go forth to war. But he had no armor. Thereupon Hephæstus came to his aid with the most beautiful suit of mail that was ever made.

Clothed in this new armor he rushed to the field and there encountered Hector. Indeed, the Trojan had reason to fear Achilles. When he was a small child his mother had plunged him into the sacred river Styx, and its waters had made his body invulnerable. But there was one place that the waters did not touch, and that was the heel and ankle by which she held him.

Hector's body, however, was liable to attack. Apollo had cautioned the Trojan prince to keep aloof and his mother and father begged him not to encounter Achilles. "It was by my command," he replied, "that the Trojans went to this day's contest. How can I therefore seek refuge for myself?" Now Achilles approached. At the sight of the Greek, Hector's courage left him and he fled. Three times Achilles chased him around the walls of Troy. At last he aimed his spear at Hector's neck and the brave Trojan fell mortally wounded. "Spare my body, and let me receive funeral rites from the sons and daughters of Troy," were his last words.

The "Iliad" closes with the death of Hector, but other poems tell us of the fate of Achilles and of those who were victorious in the end. Apollo, who disliked Achilles, gave to Paris a poisoned arrow to aim at the vulnerable heel. The arrow did its work and the bravest of warriors died in terrible agony.

But the walls of Troy still stood, and the Greeks

almost despaired of subduing the city by force. "We must take it by stratagem," said the cunning O-dys'seus (Roman name, Ulysses), and he invented a plan. A large wooden horse was constructed and filled with armed men. This the Greeks left at the gate of Troy, and they told the Trojans that it was an offering to Athene. Then they pretended to give up the siege and to sail away.

As they saw the Greek ships move from their shores the Trojans ran out from the walls of their city. They gazed in wonder at the wooden horse. "Let us take it into the city as a trophy," exclaimed one. "What madness, citizens, is this!" cried a priest of Apollo, named La-oc'o-on. "Have you not learned enough of Grecian fraud to be on your guard against it?"

Group of the Laocoon in the Vatican

He then sent a spear into the horse's side to see whether its body was hollow. Not long after that two huge serpents arose out of the sea and coiled their bodies around him and his two sons and strangled them to death. "The gods are displeased," said the Trojans. They now regarded the wooden horse as a sacred object and it was moved with solemn rites to the largest square of their city.

The Trojans now retired for the night, and the armed men within the horse seized their opportunity. When they thought the enemy were asleep, they sprang from their hiding place and opened the gates of the city for the Greeks outside to rush in. They then set fire to Troy and nearly all the Trojans perished.

This ended the siege. The wrongs of Menelaus were avenged and Helen was returned to Sparta.

Reading from Homer
Redrawn from a painting by Alma Tadema

These two great poems — the "Iliad" and the "Odyssey" — are a part of the world's literature. But how have they come down to us? Printing was not invented until the fifteenth century after the birth of Christ, and these poems were composed centuries before his birth.

In the early days of Greece there were singers or minstrels who wandered from place to place reciting stories telling of the mighty acts of the gods or the deeds of some great hero. Then there came a poet who put these myths and legends into poems, and the poet is known by the name of Homer, which means "the author." He, too, would go from place to place reciting his poems, and then other men would learn them and do the same. Thus the stories of the "Iliad" and the "Odyssey" came to be known, and later were handed down in manuscript.

Homer
From the sculpture by Bates

They have been translated into English and are not only read in our schools, but many references and allusions in our literature are from these Greek myths and legends.

THE BATTLE OF MARATHON

It was one thousand years before Christ when Homer sang of the courageous deeds of the heroes of myth and legend. More than four hundred years passed, and we hear of other heroes, not of legend and myth, but of real history. Let us see who they were and why we should remember them.

In the sixth century before Christ, Lyd'i-a in Asia

Minor was one of the great world powers. Her soil was rich in metals and her river beds contained gold. Indeed, the wealth of her king, Crœ'sus, so impressed the people of the time that even to this day his name stands for riches.

Among his subjects were the prosperous Greek cities in Asia Minor. Crœsus had favored them, and now they were ready to help him when Persia, another world power, attacked his kingdom. Persia was successful and subdued one Greek city after another until finally they all arose in revolt.

They asked the cities in Greece, their mother country, to help them, but these cities had heard of the might of Da-ri'us, "the Great King of Persia," and they had reasons to fear him. Only one came to their aid, and this city was Athens. "It is our duty to help our kinsmen," she said, and she sent them twenty ships. Away sailed the ships to Asia Minor, but it was not long before the cities were again subdued by the Persian despot. Successful in this, Darius aimed an arrow toward Athens, saying, "That city shall be punished for sending troops to Asia." Lest he should forget to do it, he ordered one of his bodyguard to say three times a day, "Master, remember the A-the'ni-ans." And indeed he did remember them.

The Great King now sent heralds to Greece to demand "earth and water"; that is, the country should recognize him as ruler over its land and water. He thought that the little city of Athens would bow in terror before him, but let us see whether it did. Some of the cities sent back "earth and water." But brave little Athens said no, and the messenger was hurled into a pit. And courageous Sparta said no, and the herald was thrown into a well.

Then what did the Great King do? He planned to attack the little Greek country. And soon occurred the first struggle in the world's history between Asia and Europe.

A great Persian army landed at the plain of Mar′a-thon near Athens. When the Athenians heard of this advance, they quickly despatched a messenger to the Spartans. Off ran the courier with the message, "Come in all haste and save Athens." But said Sparta, "You must wait a week, the law forbids us to engage in war before the full moon." And the ten thousand Athenian soldiers had to face the one hundred thousand Persians without Spartan help.

"We must march at once," said Mil-ti′a-des, the Athenian general. There was no time to wait for the full moon. From the rising ground he could see the Persian ships already in the bay of Marathon and their soldiers disembarking on the plain. At the general's command the Athenians marched down the rugged mountain roads until they came in sight of the huge army of the Persians drawn up in lines on the beach. Courage, indeed, was needed to face these hitherto unconquered foes.

Miltiades

But what did the Persians see? Not linen tunics and wicker shields, not darts and light scimiters; but heavy bronze armor and long spears. The soldiers of Athens were not only equipped for the fight; they were men of undaunted courage.

Now Miltiades hastily formed his ranks and ordered the charge. With their spears pointed, down rushed the Athenians. Soon there was a clash of arms and the Persian wings gave way. Another charge — this time upon the Persian center; another fierce struggle and the enemy were driven in confusion to their ships. "Burn them, burn the ships," was the command. And before they could set sail, seven Persian ships were burned. More than six thousand of the enemy perished in this battle, while the Athenian loss was not two hundred. At the close of the battle, it is said, one of the soldiers, named Eucles, covered with blood and wounds, ran to Athens to tell the joyful news. Almost exhausted with fighting, he was soon so weary that he could scarcely keep on his feet; but he struggled on. When he came to the edge of the city the people gathered around him. He reeled and fell dying to the ground. As he fell he said faintly, "Rejoice, we triumph," and the next moment he was dead.

The battle of Marathon, which occurred 490 B.C., is regarded as one of the decisive battles of the world, for that victory encouraged the Athenians to fight to the last, whatever might be the result. "The Athenians succeed," wrote a Greek historian one hundred years later, "because they throw themselves into whatever they resolve to do."

Now there was no need for a slave to say, "Master,

remember the Athenians." The Great King remembered them only too well. He took an oath that neither he nor his successors should rest until Greece was conquered. But as Darius was planning another invasion, he suddenly died.

LEONIDAS AND THE THREE HUNDRED

Greece was left alone for more than five years. Then Xerx'es, the son of the Great King, declared, "My father's oath must be fulfilled." This had hardly been said when he led an army of half a million soldiers, with a fleet of more than a thousand ships, to finish the work that Darius had begun.

When they heard of his coming, Sparta and Athens called a meeting to discuss plans for defense. Some of the Greek states refused to send representatives; they were jealous of Athens and Sparta. There was reason for alarm. Athens had sent a messenger to Delphi to see what the priestess of Apollo would advise. "When everything else in the land shall be taken," said the oracle, "Zeus grants to Athene that the wooden wall alone shall remain undestroyed, and it shall defend you and your children." What did this mean?

A brave man who was known as The-mis'to-cles the Ready said that the wooden wall meant their ships, and he urged Athens to build a fleet. "A country like Greece, surrounded by seas, must assert herself on the waters," he said. "The city needs no ships," replied others; "they are useless expense." But it was not long before Athens became the greatest naval power in Greece.

When Xerxes and his great host came to the shore of the Hellespont, a narrow strait between Europe and Asia, he ordered his engineers to build two bridges, so that his army might cross the strait. The bridges were built, but a storm arose and destroyed them. And what did the angry king do? He commanded his generals to scourge the strait three hundred times, to teach the waters that he was their master. Then new bridges were built, and so great was the Persian army that it took them seven days and seven nights to pass over these bridges.

Xerxes and his host soon entered Greece and reached a high mountain. Not far away, between the cliff and the sea, was the narrow pass of Ther-mop′y-læ, guarded by Le-on′i-das, the king of Sparta. With him were three hundred Spartans and three thousand soldiers from other Greek states. When the allies saw the great Persian army advancing, they cried, "We had best retreat." "Let not a man stir," said Leonidas.

The Persian army then sent swift riders in advance to see whether the pass was guarded. The couriers returned with the report, "We saw there bold men who were combing their long hair." "They are an easy prey," said Xerxes; "men who have time to give so much attention to dress are readily mastered." "But, O King," exclaimed the couriers, "they are Spartans, and it is accounted shameful at Sparta to go down into battle with uncombed hair." Then Xerxes ordered that the long-haired Spartans be brought to him alive. But this was no easy task. The Spartans and the allies stood their ground. The king of Persia at last sent an entire division of his army to try to force the pass. Again and again the Persians charged, but that solid line stood more firmly than before, and at sunset from his throne on the rocks, Xerxes saw that many of his men had fallen.

The next morning another charge was ordered, and again the Greek spears did their work. "Bid the Immortals charge," then commanded the angry king. They were his royal bodyguard, and it was said of them that they could not be defeated. With their silver and gold-hilted lances the Immortals dashed against the Spartan spears, but their shining armor did not force the pass.

When Xerxes saw that his favorites were driven back, he groaned in agony. It was now past sunset of the second day, and the Greeks were holding their position as firmly as ever. But in the darkness of night there crept a traitor to the Persian king telling him of a path by which his force could fall upon the Greeks. A deserter brought the news to Leonidas. "Let us retreat before the Persians attack us on both sides at once," urged some of the Greeks. "The laws of Sparta bid her men to conquer or die," replied Leonidas. "For my part I shall obey her laws." And this was also the answer of the three hundred Spartans who were with him.

They did not wait for the Persians to advance, but

they met the enemy and rushed upon them. It was a daring thing to do, and soon the brave Leonidas fell, and with him his three hundred Spartans. Later their names were engraved on a pillar and placed in a public square in Sparta, so that other Greeks might read and imitate their bravery. And at Thermopylæ a monument in the shape of a lion was raised, and a pillar with the words:

"Go, passer-by, at Sparta tell,
  Obedient to her law we fell."

SALAMIS

The taking of Thermopylæ gave Xerxes an open road to Athens. As the oracle at Delphi had predicted that the Greek city would be destroyed, the Athenians hastily boarded their ships, and thus sought protection behind their "wooden walls."

Their great statesman, Themistocles, was eager to encounter the enemy on the waters. "Those who begin a race before the signal are scourged," he was told. "That is true," said Themistocles, "but the laggards never win a crown."

The oracle had said that Athens was doomed, and it was not long before the Persian army entered the deserted city and burned it. Now the only hope of the Athenians was in their fleet off the island of Sal′a-mis. Not far away was the magnificent armada of the Persians. Xerxes was proud of the fleet that he had brought safely into Grecian waters, and he ordered a throne to be built on a high cliff so that he could see his ships destroy the little Grecian fleet.

Morning dawned and the Greeks were in the bay with the enemy in front of them, and Xerxes was on his throne ready for the battle. The fleets were soon face to face, and the fight began. For a time it seemed as if the Persians would win. But later, ship was dashed against ship and the proud Xerxes saw one vessel after another of his fleet destroyed. The conflict lasted from dawn until night. The Persians had twice as many ships, but the fierce attacks of the Greeks finally won the victory.

Although a Spartan commanded the Greek fleet, Athens knew that the honor for the victory at Salamis belonged to Themistocles the Ready. Greek courage had saved Greece from the slavery of the East; it had done more than this, it had saved Europe from the rule of despots. If the Persian hordes had conquered Greece, they might have subdued all Europe and destroyed the growing civilization that afterward was transplanted to America. It is true then, as an American historian has said, that it was our battles that the brave Greeks fought at Marathon, Thermopylæ, and Salamis — the battles of law and liberty.

THE CITY WALL

Xerxes had not yet abandoned the hope of conquering the Greeks. He left his brother-in-law, Mardo'ni-us, in Greece with a splendid army to see what he could do. This satrap tried to persuade the Athenians to desert the other Greek states and to become an ally of Persia. "So long as the sun holds his course, we will never be friends to Xerxes," they replied. "Great as may be his power, Athens trusts to the aid of the gods and heroes whose temples he has burnt."

In the meantime the Spartans had raised an army under the command of their king. They met the Persians near the city of Pla-te′a and there defeated them. Mardonius was killed. The Persian camp was sacked and wagonloads of silver and gold vessels and rich armor fell into the possession of the Greeks. The battle of Platea ended the Persian invasion of Greece.

The Spartans marveled at the richness they saw in the Persian tents, and the king asked the slaves of Mardonius to prepare a meal such as they would provide for their master. When he saw the splendor of the feast — the gold and silver dishes, the rich cushions and carpets — he exclaimed, "How absurd to go on a conquering expedition with all these encumbrances." And it is said that he refused to partake of the feast, but sat down to the plain Spartan meal. This splendor was not only in the Persian tents, but it was seen in the countless chariots, in the rich, glittering armor of the Immortals, in the burnished helmets of the soldiers, and in the silken canopies over the grandees.

The Athenians now went back to Athens, but they found a ruined town — their houses and temples burned to the ground. They felt that their goddess Athene, the defender of their capital, had deserted them. But later what did they see? The olive tree, which she created when they named the city after her, was shooting out a long branch from its blackened trunk, and on the branch leaves were budding forth. "Our goddess is still with us," they joyfully exclaimed, and they interpreted the budding leaves as a sign to rebuild their city.

At once the people of Athens went to work to build up their houses, and it was not long before they were provided with new homes. "Let us build a wall and so strengthen our capital that we may not be driven out again," said Themistocles the Ready.

Acropolis at Athens, in present condition

This had hardly been said when every Athenian who could lift a block or push a barrow was working on the fortification. The wall was to be not only around the city, but it was to extend to her ports four miles away, and thus in time of war provisions could be brought in safety from her harbor.

When Sparta heard that Athens was fortifying herself, she tried to prevent it. She was jealous and desired to be mistress of Greece. "We will build our wall and not have any words with the Spartans," said the Athenians. And the great wall sixty feet high, with huge stones projecting here and there, was built, and it stood for many, many years; but to-day no trace of it is left.

PERICLES AND ATHENS

It was about 460 B.C. when Per'i-cles became the leader in Athens. He was a favorite with the people, and through his influence some wise laws were passed. "If anyone is accused of a crime, he should have a trial before a body of citizens," said Pericles. This was like the trial by jury to-day in our country. Then, too, he said that any Athenian employed in the army or navy should be paid for his services. But this was not all that Pericles accomplished. He not only strengthened Athens, but he beautified it. It has been well said that he found the city of brick and left it of marble.

Pericles
From bust in the British Museum

In the center of the town was a great square-topped hill, rising to a height of two hundred feet. It was called the Ac-rop'o-lis, from two Greek words meaning "city height." It had been the ancient citadel of Athens, and there the early Athenian kings sat in judgment and assembled their councils. Later there were temples and houses erected on the hill, but the Persians had destroyed them. Now Pericles advised that on this Acropolis the Athenians should build a marble temple to their goddess Athene Parthenos (which means "the maiden Athene").

Architects and sculptors from all parts of Greece came to Athens for work. The most famous sculptor of his age was Phid'i-as, a friend of Pericles, and he it was who designed the Par'then-on, the marble temple of Athene. It was begun in 447 B.C. and it was completed in 438 B.C. It had a very beautiful colonnade of forty-six fluted columns, each thirty-five feet high, supporting the gabled roof. Within the colonnade were the solid walls enclosing two rooms, the chamber and the treasury of the goddess. It is said that the workmanship of the unseen parts was as perfect as that of the parts which were seen. In front of the temple was the great bronze statue of Athene, the work of Phidias. The goddess was represented

The "Winged Victory"
Statue in the Louvre, Paris

as the defender of the city, and the polished tip of her spear glittering in the sun could be seen by the mariner far out at sea, as he sailed toward Athens.

The Parthenon was one of the wonders of the world; for nearly a thousand years it was the glorious temple to the Greek goddess. Later it was converted into a Christian church, and still later into a Mo-ham'me-dan mosque. In the latter part of the seventeenth century it was used by the Turks as a powder magazine. Then an explosion

Parthenon at Athens (present condition)

occurred which destroyed the building and left only a ruined colonnade. Pieces of the Parthenon sculpture are still seen in the ruins or in the Acropolis Museum. Other pieces were carried away and later acquired by an Englishman who bought them for the British Museum. But the splendid statues of Phidias have been destroyed. Copies of them have come down to us, and these furnish studies for artists and sculptors of our day.

It is supposed that the bronze statue known as the Lemnian Athene was the work of Phidias. It was dedicated on the Acropolis by the Athenian colonists who had received free land in Lemnos. The beautiful head of this statue is now in Bo-lo'gna.

Another great sculptor of Athens was Myron. He and Phidias studied under the same master. A copy of his bronze statue the Discus-thrower was found in Rome and is now in the Vatican, the residence of the Pope. But the most generally admired Greek statue is Aphrodite of Melos (The Venus of Milo). We do not know who carved her beautiful figure. The statue was discovered in 1820 in a cave on the island of Melos, off the coast of Greece, and it is now in the Louvre, the great art gallery of Paris.

Hermes
Detail of statue by Praxiteles

The most famous pupil of Phidias was Prax-it'el-es, an Athenian. He carved a beautiful statue of Hermes for the temple of Hera at Olympia. Hermes was the herald of Zeus, and the Greek sculptor represented him as taking his little brother Di-on'y-sus (the god of wine) to the nymphs to be reared by them.

On the southeast slope of the Acropolis was the theater of Dionysus, named after the god of wine because the drama originated in the songs and dances in honor of Dionysus. The rising seats of the theater were cut in a semicircle into the rocky hill. There was no roof; it was an open air theater, and the spectators could look beyond the stage across the blue Ægean Sea. Twice a year the masterpieces of the great Greek dramatists—Æs'chy-lus, Eu-rip'i-des, and Soph'o-cles—were presented. The performance began early in the morning and lasted all day. If a citizen was too poor to attend, Pericles secured for him an admission fee from the public treasury. The object of the theater was to educate, and largely through the influence of Pericles the theater became one of the most important institutions of Athens. The University of California has erected a beautiful open-air theater modeled after the theater of Dionysus.

Bust of Dionysus, Naples

On the western side of the Acropolis, from the Parthenon to the city, was a marble stairway of sixty steps. There were other splendid buildings erected in Athens — the The-se'um, a temple in memory of their ancient king, The'se-us; the Mu-se'um, where the young Athenians studied the arts sacred to the muses; the schools for the philosophers, which were colonnades of pillars supporting roofs to give protection from the sun. Besides the beautiful architecture there were the gardens of the Academy, dotted with statues, and the olive groves of the Ly-ce'um just outside the city walls.

Pericles was at the head of Athens for nearly thirty years, and in that time the city had reason to be proud of herself. She then reached the height of her glory in art, and her masterpieces in sculpture have never been surpassed.

THE GREEK BOY

The houses of the Greeks were built around paved courts. In the middle of the court was a fountain and there was also an altar to the hero ancestor of the master of the house. This forefather was the guardian of the household, and before each meal offerings were made to him and wine poured out. The rooms of the houses were little occupied, for the Greeks enjoyed living in the open air.

The Athenian child was in the care of a nurse until his seventh year. Then he was given into the charge of a trusted servant called a pedagogue (the word means "conductor of children"). At the age of seven the boy entered school accompanied by his pedagogue, whose duty it was to see that no harm would come to the youth on his way to school. He attended by turns the school for grammar, the school for gymnastics, and the school for music. In the first he was taught reading, writing, and the stories of Homer.

About the middle of the sixth century B.C. Pi-sis tra-tus, a ruler of Athens, collected and arranged the poems of Homer and had them written down, after which no Greek was thought to be educated unless he thoroughly knew the "Iliad" and the "Odyssey." Before the time of Pisistratus there had been no written copy of these poems.

The teacher in the school for grammar was called the grammarian. He often gave his lessons in the streets and on the public squares.

In the school for gymnastics the youth received his instruction in physical training. This training began with the child and continued through old age. The exercises were wrestling, boxing, running, throwing the discus or quoit, fencing, and using the spear. The Athenian tried to overcome any physical defect or awkwardness, and no day was passed without some time being spent in the development of the body. In Greek art we see this perfection of the body expressed in marble and in color. Solon, one of the wise law-makers of Athens, placed physical and intellectual training upon the same footing. "Children," he said, "should above everything else learn to swim and to read."

The Discus Thrower
Statue by Myron

In the school for music the youth was taught to sing

and to play upon the stringed instrument, the lyre. The master would sing the song first, and then the pupil, and if the youth made mistakes he was often severely punished.

The instruction in grammar, gymnastics, and music was for the wealthier class of citizens. The poorer class learned only reading, swimming, and a trade.

In Sparta it was the law that when a child was born the father must take it before a council of old men, who examined the little stranger. If it was found not to be strong, the child was taken from its mother and carried off to a mountain, where it died of hunger and exposure. If the council decided that the child was healthy, it was returned to the mother and remained in her care until it was seven years of age. Then the state took charge of the youth.

To be a perfect soldier was the Spartan's aim and ambition. He was never to turn his back in battle. As the son went off to war his mother gave him a shield saying, "With it or on it." That is, he was not to throw it away in flight, but bring it home honorably or be borne upon it as a dead warrior.

The Spartan cared little for art and literature, but music and gymnastics were cultivated. Once a year there was an exhibition, where the youth showed the perfection of his physical condition and his skill in bodily movement.

The Spartan boy was taught to read and to write, but above all, he learned to endure pain, to obey orders, to be respectful to his elders, not to speak unless spoken to, and then his answers were to be as short as possible. He went barefoot even in the coldest weather, he ate the plainest and coarsest food, and he slept on rushes and reeds which he had gathered by the river.

He was trained even to steal, for in war he would often have to commit theft or go without food. The youth was praised if he could steal without being discovered; but if caught, he was punished. Nothing, however, deserved more merit than bearing pain without complaint. He who could do without food the longest, who could bear the most whipping without crying, was indeed to be envied. His courage was tested at the temple of Artemis, where he was thrashed severely. And it is said that many a Spartan boy allowed himself to be flogged to death rather than to complain. The story is told of a little fellow who stole a young fox and hid it under his tunic for fear of being discovered. The imprisoned fox began to gnaw at the boy's chest, but the little fellow did not utter a groan or a cry, and the fox finally bit him to death. And to-day we use the phrase "brave as a Spartan."

The Spartan youth would often be questioned by his elders and the boy was required to make his answers brief and forceful. And our term "laconic," referring to a short, effective answer, comes from Laconia, another name for Sparta.

Respect for old age was probably the most commendable lesson that the Spartan youth was taught. It is said that at one time an aged man entered an assembly of Greeks. The Athenians laughed at him, but every Spartan arose and offered him a seat. "The Athenians know politeness," said the old man, "but the Spartans practise it."

We thus see that at Sparta physical strength and military skill were the qualities most desired; while at Athens, although the body was not neglected, the chief attention was given to the cultivation of the mind.

THE OLYMPIC GAMES

There was a great festival that both Spartan and Athenian attended, as well as Greeks from other states — the Olympic Games. There were many joyous celebrations, with games, held in the different cities of Greece, but the Olympic festival was the most famous.

It was held in honor of their great god Zeus, in mid-

Zeus
From a bust in the Vatican, Rome

summer, each fourth year, at Olympia in Élis, a state northwest of Sparta. During the interval when these games took place a sacred truce was observed throughout Greece, arms were laid aside, and all hostilities between the Greek states were suspended for a time. The four-year period was known as an O-lym′pi-ad, and this became a unit in counting time. Events were dated from the first recorded Olympiad, which went back to 776 B.C., when a certain athlete won the foot race — a dash of more than two hundred yards. For example, we might say that an event occurred in Washington's administration; the Greeks would say that it happened in the fifth Olympiad.

At Olympia was an ancient temple for the worship of Zeus. It was said to have been built by the mighty Her'cu-les, the son of Zeus, who was noted for manly strength and patient endurance. Later the temple was adorned with beautiful sculptures. In the sacred chamber stood the great statue of Zeus — the masterpiece of Phidias. It was forty feet high and placed on a twelve-foot pedestal. The god of gods was represented as seated on his throne, which was made of cedar and decorated with gold and precious stones. His body was of ivory, with drapery and ornaments of fine gold. His brow was crowned with a wreath of olive, and in his right hand he held his scepter.

The legend tells us that Hercules not only built the temple, but he founded the Olympic Games in honor of Zeus, and it was said that he acted as umpire at the first festival.

At these games there were contests in running, jumping, hurling the spear, throwing the quoit, wrestling, boxing. Then there were also chariot races and horse races.

The judges gave to each winner a palm branch, and on the last day of the festival they placed a wreath of olive from the sacred tree of Hercules upon the victor's head. But the highest honor that could come to any competitor was to be proclaimed "four-years champion of Greece."

On his return to his native city the champion was greeted as a conquering hero and a life-size statue of him was placed in the grove at Olympia. The Athenians did even more than this — they pensioned their champion for life and their poets sang his praises.

The most talented men in Greece came to the Olympic festival. The poet, the musician, the philosopher, the historian were all there, entertaining the people between the games. He-rod'o-tus, the "Father of History," would read his "History of the Persian War," and Pindar, the great poet, would recite his odes. And the people were always a ready audience eager to hear and see what was new in poetry and song.

The Olympic Games continued for more than three centuries after the birth of Christ. In recent years there has been an effort made to revive them. Representatives from different nations met and formed an international Olympic Committee. At the suggestion of this committee a series of festivals was begun, the games to be four years apart as in the old Greek times. It was arranged that the first of the series should be held in Athens in 1896; the second in Paris, 1900; the third, in St. Louis, 1904; the fourth in London, 1908, and the fifth in Stockholm in 1912. Some of the old contests of Greece were revived, such as throwing the discus and the javelin, and above all, the Marathon race. In 1896 this race was won by a Greek, but in 1908 by an American.

Infant Hercules
Sculpture in the Louvre, Paris

CHAPTER III

RULERS OF GREECE

THE Olympic Games gave the independent states of Greece something in common. And it was a good thing that they were thus brought together, for often the states were jealous of one another and quarrels among them were frequent. The states of Greece were not united by a common government. Some of them were ruled by kings, others by a few men who had all the power; such states were called oligarchies.

THE GOVERNMENT OF ATHENS

In ancient times Athens had been a kingdom. One of her early kings was Theseus, and his descendants ruled for many years. Then a people from the north invaded the state, and the contest was decided by a duel. The Athenian champion won and he was made king. At his death Codrus, his son, became ruler. Now another tribe, the Do'ri-ans, invaded Athens. The oracle at Delphi had said, "If the Dorians slay the Athenian king, they shall come to sorrow." The battle began, and the Dorians were indeed careful not to touch King Codrus. "What does this strange conduct mean?"

asked the king. And he was told what the priestess at Delphi had said. Then Codrus threw off his royal dress and put on the garb of a common soldier and appeared before the enemy's camp. He defied the sentinels, and they, not knowing that he was the Athenian king, struck him dead. When the Dorians heard what had happened they quickly left their tents and hurried home.

The Delphic Oracle
From a Greek vase

The Athenians grieved for their brave ruler. "Athens shall have no more kings," they said. They thought they would thus honor Codrus, who had sacrificed his life for the state, and that no one less noble should wear the title. After that their ruler was called an archon, and he was elected from the family of Codrus for a term of ten years.

Later a body of nine archons was chosen from the nobility, and they were elected annually. The first archon had charge of the family rights, such as marriages and the fortunes of heiresses. The second was judge in cases of murder, and he was also the guardian of strangers in the city. The other six presided as judges in less important cases. The people had no voice in the government. There were no written laws, and the archons were enriching themselves at the expense of the state.

The people then demanded that the laws be published so that they would know whether the archons were ruling with justice. Accordingly Draco, one of the archons, drew up a written code of laws, and they were engraved on wooden blocks and set up in public places, where all might read them. "These laws are written in blood," said the people. The least offense was considered a crime, and there was the death penalty for stealing even a cabbage. The people were not contented, and they drove Draco out of Athens.

SOLON

Later Solon was chosen first archon. He altered the laws and wrote them on tablets and placed them in the public squares. The Athenians were pleased. "Solon is the wisest man that ever lived," they said. Only those who owned property could be elected to office, and they were elected every year in a general assembly of all the people. As it was not convenient for the

Solon

people to meet frequently, they delegated their power to a council (senate) of four hundred members. But when there was a question pertaining to war or peace, the General Assembly voted; and if a man was thought to be dangerous to the state, the people had the power to banish him.

But this was not all that Solon did. He established a Court of Justice consisting of archons and ex-archons, which heard and decided cases involving capital punishment. This court met on the hill of Ares and was called the Ar′e-op′a-gus (Ares' hill), and it became one of the most respected of ancient courts.

Solon had ruled for some time and he now desired to go on a long journey. But before he went he made the people of Athens promise that they would not change the laws for ten years.

On his journey he visited the rich Crœsus in Lyd′i-a. The proud monarch showed him all the splendor of his kingdom. He then asked, "Who is the happiest of men?" "An honest man," replied Solon, "who lived uprightly, was neither rich nor poor, had good children, and died bravely for his country." "Who is the next happiest?" inquired Crœsus. "Two brothers," answered the Athenian, "who were so loving and dutiful to their mother that when she desired to go to the temple of Hera, they yoked themselves to her car and drew her thither, then having given this proof of their love, they lay down to sleep, and so died without pain or grief." "And what do you think of me?" then asked the rich monarch, much annoyed. "Ah," said Solon, "call no man happy until you see the end of his life."

There happened to be at the court of Crœsus an Egyp′tian slave named Æsop, who gave his advice in fables. This was the same Æsop whose fables of the wolf and the lamb, the fox and the grapes, the crow and the pitcher, we know to-day. And when Æsop saw the displeasure of Crœsus he said, "Visits to kings should be seldom or else pleasant." "No," replied Solon, "visits to kings should be seldom or else profitable."

After many years of absence, Solon returned to Athens and he found his nephew Pisistratus ruling with unlimited power. In those days such a ruler was called a tyrant, whether he ruled well or ill. Although Pisistratus belonged to the aristocracy (from Greek words meaning "rule by rich men"), he sided with the poor, and he did some good things for Athens. He collected the poems of Homer, he opened his library to the public, he improved the roads and laid out a public park, the Lyceum, just outside the city walls. At his death his sons succeeded him, but they were not popular; one was killed and the other was forced to leave the state.

Æsop
Redrawn from the painting by Velasques in Museum, Madrid

Later Clis'the-nes, a nobleman, proposed a series of changes in Solon's constitution. Holding property was no longer to be a qualification for office. The rich and the poor, the nobleman and the commoner, could share in the government. Clisthenes divided the state into one hundred districts which had a local self-government with a head corresponding to our mayor. He next divided the districts among ten new tribes. These met in a general assembly ten times a year on a hill west of the Acropolis. It was not convenient for all the tribes to meet so often in Athens, so each tribe selected a delegation of fifty men, and these made up the Council of Five Hundred. There were still the nine archons who were elected annually, and there was also the Areopagus, the Court of Justice.

Athens thus became a democracy (from the Greek meaning "rule by the people"), and this was her government when Pericles became leader. A Greek historian has well said that during that great period of her glory Athens was a democracy in name only; in reality she was ruled by her ablest citizen.

THE STORY OF SOCRATES

At no period in the history of Athens was public speaking so popular as in the Golden Age of Pericles (B.C. 464–429). The Sophists, a class of philosophers, would go from place to place teaching the art of public speaking, and they would charge high rates for their tuition. Since by clever argument they often made the worse appear the better reason — error appear truth, and injustice, justice — their instruction came to mean arguing with the intention of deceiving. And to-day the term "sophistry" means deceptive reasoning.

But the greatest of the philosophers (lovers of wisdom) was Soc′ra-tes. He was not a Sophist. He did not pretend to have wisdom, although he was the wisest of men. He was always studying and asking questions, trying to find out the exact truth about everything. He had many followers among the young men, and he would teach them in the groves or in the market-place or on the corners of the streets. He would not take pay for his teaching, although he was poor. He went barefoot and wore the same threadbare coat all the year round.

He was not attractive in appearance—he had a large, bald head, thick lips, bulging eyes, and a flat nose. He was gentle, however, and he bore his hardships without ever murmuring. Even his scolding wife, Xan-tip′pe, could not make him angry. Although by nature he had a violent temper, he had learned to control it. To-day her name stands for a scold. Once she became so impatient that she threw a jug of water on him. But he smilingly replied, "I have often observed, Xantippe, that rain follows thunder."

The priestess at Delphi had said, "Socrates is the wisest man in Greece." "This cannot be true," replied the philosopher, "for I know, myself, that I know nothing." And he soon discovered by cross-questioning that the Sophists were more ignorant than he, for he knew that he did not know, while they would never admit their ignorance. He would not only question the Sophists, but men in every walk of life — statesmen and soldiers, artists and shopkeepers. He would first ask them to express their views on a subject, and then by questioning them he would reveal their errors. And to-day this method of questioning is called Socratic, after the Greek philosopher.

Socrates had many friends, but he had also many

enemies who were jealous of him. And one of these enemies was Ar′is-toph′a-nes, a writer of comic plays. He wrote a comedy and called it "The Clouds." The gods mentioned in it were not those of Mount Olympus, but the Clouds, the Air, and the Tongue. And it was not necessary to tell the Athenians whom the teacher

Masks worn by Greek Actors

and the pupil in the play represented. They were well marked by the masks which the actors wore. In those days public men were frequently ridiculed on the stage. And this time there was no mistaking the characters. They were intended for Socrates and his pupil Al′ci-bi′a-des. The pupil was represented as an attractive young man who, advised by his teacher, bought horses and then cheated his creditors. He not only treated his father with disrespect, but also Zeus and Athene.

It is said that Socrates once attended the play, and he was asked why he went. "To see the faults of which I am accused," was his answer. "There may be some that I can correct."

"The Clouds" amused the Athenians at the theater Dionysus for more than twenty years; they would talk about the play and laugh at the jokes.

Alcibiades had been a favorite with the people, but there came a time when he turned traitor, and then the Athenians said, "Aristophanes is right, Socrates has corrupted our young men."

The philosopher was nearly seventy years of age

when there appeared a charge against him — accusing him of teaching disrespect to the gods and ruining young men. There were many stories about the gods and goddesses that Socrates did not believe. And although he never heard of the true God, he knew there must be a wise Being who governs the world and knows all things.

Finally there were orders for his arrest, and he was brought before the council of the Areopagus to plead his own cause. "Because I am thought to have some power of teaching youth, O my judges," he said, "is that a reason why I should suffer death? I have always told young men to be good and virtuous. I have never turned the gods into ridicule, for it is wrong to make fun of anything which is regarded as sacred by others. My whole life is the best defense that I can offer." But the judges did not listen to his plea and he was sentenced to death.

The death penalty, however, could not be carried out for thirty days, as a ship had just set sail for Delos bearing offerings to Apollo, and it was the law that no one could be put to death while this ship was on its way either going or returning. Socrates therefore remained in prison during this time. His friends were allowed to visit him, and he talked to them about his death. He told them to love virtue and to do right,

A Greek Altar

and not to repay evil with evil. "I cannot bear to think of your dying innocent," said Crito, one of his pupils. "What!" exclaimed Socrates, "would you think it better for me to die guilty?"

The ship had now returned, and at sunset Socrates was to drink the hemlock, a deadly poison. "Let us bribe the jailer," said the anxious Crito. "It is against the law," replied Socrates, "and I have never disobeyed the law." And he told his pupils not to forget the lessons that he had taught them. He then calmly drank the hemlock, and soon sleep overtook him, and thus he died.

His greatest pupil was Plato, who not only recorded the last conversations of Socrates, but continued the teaching of his master. "Thus," said Plato, "died the man who, of all with whom we were acquainted, was in death the noblest, in life the wisest and best."

THE BOYHOOD OF ALEXANDER THE GREAT

Plato's greatest pupil was Ar'is-tot-le, who was the teacher of Alexander, the King of Mac'e-do'ni-a, a country north of Greece. Alexander was the son of King Philip II, who had successfully invaded Greece and who was recognized as that country's champion against its old enemy, Persia. Philip had caused one Greek city to go against another. "Suppose that you have one of the gods as surety that Philip will leave you untouched," said De-mos'the-nes to the Athenian Assembly, "in the name of the gods, it is a shame for you to sacrifice the rest of Greece." Demosthenes was the greatest of Greek orators, and those orations in the Athenian Assembly we know to-day as the "Philippics." Philip was assassinated, however, before he could begin the invasion of Asia.

Alexander was only twenty years of age when he

THE BOYHOOD OF ALEXANDER THE GREAT

succeeded his father to the throne. As a boy he was known for his will power; whatever he set out to do he was determined to accomplish. A beautiful black horse had been brought to the King of Macedon, but the animal was balky and he would let no one mount him. "That horse is wild and untrained," said Philip, and he ordered him to be taken away. "No," exclaimed Alexander, "the attendants have not the skill to handle the animal. He is too good a horse for those men to spoil in that way." "What do you mean by criticizing your elders as if you were wiser than they," demanded Philip, "or know so much more about handling horses than they do?" "I can manage him better than anyone else," was the reply, "if you will only give me a chance." "But if you don't succeed, what penalty are you willing to pay for your boldness?" asked the king. "I'll pay the price of the horse," was the answer.

Demosthenes

The bystanders laughed at him, but that did not daunt the young prince. He walked up to the animal, took him by the bridle, and turned his head toward the sun, for he had observed that the horse was afraid of his own shadow. The youth stroked him gently, and when he had somewhat subdued him, he sprang into the saddle and started off at full speed. It was not long before he came galloping back, and as he dismounted, his father kissed him and said, "My son, seek thee a kingdom suited to thy powers; Macedonia is not broad enough for thee."

Alexander training Bucephalos

The young prince was always eager to do something. At one time when news came that Philip had won a great battle and had captured a city, Alexander exclaimed to several of his playfellows, "Father will get everything in advance, boys; he will not leave any great task for me to share with you."

It is said that once during the king's absence the youth entertained a body of special ambassadors from the Persian court. The conversation of the boy aroused the admiration of the Persians. He asked them about the length of their roads, the methods of land travel, what kind of soldier the Shah was, how large was the Persian army, and what made Persia a great empire.

When Alexander was twelve years of age he was sent to Aristotle's school, which was held in a grove. There he met the sons of other kings. The master would often walk with his pupils in the shady paths, instructing them all the while. He taught them the poems of Homer, and it is said that Alexander could recite the "Iliad" from beginning to end. Aristotle would tell his pupils to be true and brave and to cultivate noble friendships. One day he asked them, "When you become king in your father's stead, what favor do you think you will show me, your old teacher?" "You shall dine at my table," said one of the princes, " and I will make the court show you honor and respect." "I will make you my chief treasurer," answered another, "and I will consult you as adviser in all that is brought me for decision." And then Aristotle turned to Alexander and asked, "My son, what do you propose to do with me, your old teacher, when you come to sit upon the throne of your father, Philip?" "What right have you to ask me such questions about that which the future has yet to bring?" was the reply. "As I have no assurance of the morrow, I can only say when the day is come; then I will give you answer." "Well said," exclaimed Aristotle; "thou wilt one day be the greatest king of all."

THE CONQUESTS OF ALEXANDER

And now let us see whether this prophecy was fulfilled. Like his father, Alexander turned his attention to an attack upon Persia. But he first visited the chief cities of Greece, to let them know that he was their master. At Corinth he called upon Di-og'e-nes, who belonged to a class of philosophers called Cynics (from the Greek word meaning "a dog"). The Cynics ridiculed the actions of men. Alexander found Diogenes sitting in a huge earthenware tub. He introduced himself, "I am Alexander the King." "And I am Diogenes the Cynic," was the reply. "Can I do anything for you, Diogenes?" asked Alexander. "Only stand out of my sunshine," growled the Cynic. And as the king went away he exclaimed, "If I were not Alexander, I would be Diogenes." He no doubt meant that if he were not to become master of the world, he would prefer to be the Cynic who despised earthly things.

Greek Horsemen
From the Parthenon

Alexander was now ready to attack Persia, and in the spring (334 B.C.) he landed in Asia Minor with more than thirty-five thousand Greeks and Macedonians. He soon met a Persian army much larger than his own. A terrible battle was fought; Alexander won, and it was not long before he became master of Asia Minor.

In the town of Gordium he entered a temple where

THE CONQUESTS OF ALEXANDER

was the sacred chariot of old King Gordius. The yoke of the chariot was fastened to the pole by a knot of tough fiber. "He who can untie that knot," declared the oracle, "will become the master of Asia." But Alexander did not try to untie it, he cut it with one stroke of his sword. The people looked upon the deed as an unfavorable omen. "He will become our master," they said. And to-day we apply the term "Gordian knot" to any difficulty demanding decided action.

Later, on his march, Alexander met a queen of a certain province, who desired to adopt him as her son. She begged him to take all her best cooks with him to provide his meals for the future. "No," said Alexander, "my master, Aristotle, has given me the best recipe for an appetite." "What is it?" inquired the queen. "A march before daybreak as the sauce for my dinner," answered the king, "and a light dinner as the sauce for my supper."

He told his soldiers not to plunder the country, for it belonged to him, and that the people were as much his subjects as they were. He then marched south and defeated a Persian army of six hundred thousand led by their king. The Persian monarch made his escape, but his wife, mother, and children were taken captives, and it is said that Alexander treated them with respect and kindness. He now took the title of King of Persia. It was not long before he

Osiris
An Egyptian god

entered Egypt and was welcomed by the people, who were tired of Persian rule. Here he founded Alexandria, which later became the foremost city of the world.

He then marched southeast into unknown country and led his army over great deserts into the plains of northern India. It is said that he treated honorably the people he conquered. The Indian king, Porus, made a bold stand, but he was finally overpowered and captured. Alexander asked him how he expected to be treated. "Like a king," was the reply. "That you certainly shall be," said Alexander.

His soldiers were so worn out with marching that when they reached the banks of the Hy'pha-sis they refused to go farther, and Alexander was compelled to return homeward. He thought that he had reached nearly the end of the world. The return journey was not easy over burning sands in the scorching heat of a noonday sun. Often the soldiers' thirst could not be satisfied. At one time a little water was brought to Alexander, but he poured it away and said, "I do not care to take what all cannot share."

The Emblem of Persia

They at last reached Bab'y-lon, one of the capitals of the Persian Empire, and Alexander decided to make this city the seat of his mighty kingdom. He adopted many Persian customs. Seated on his golden throne, he received ambassadors from every known people in Europe and

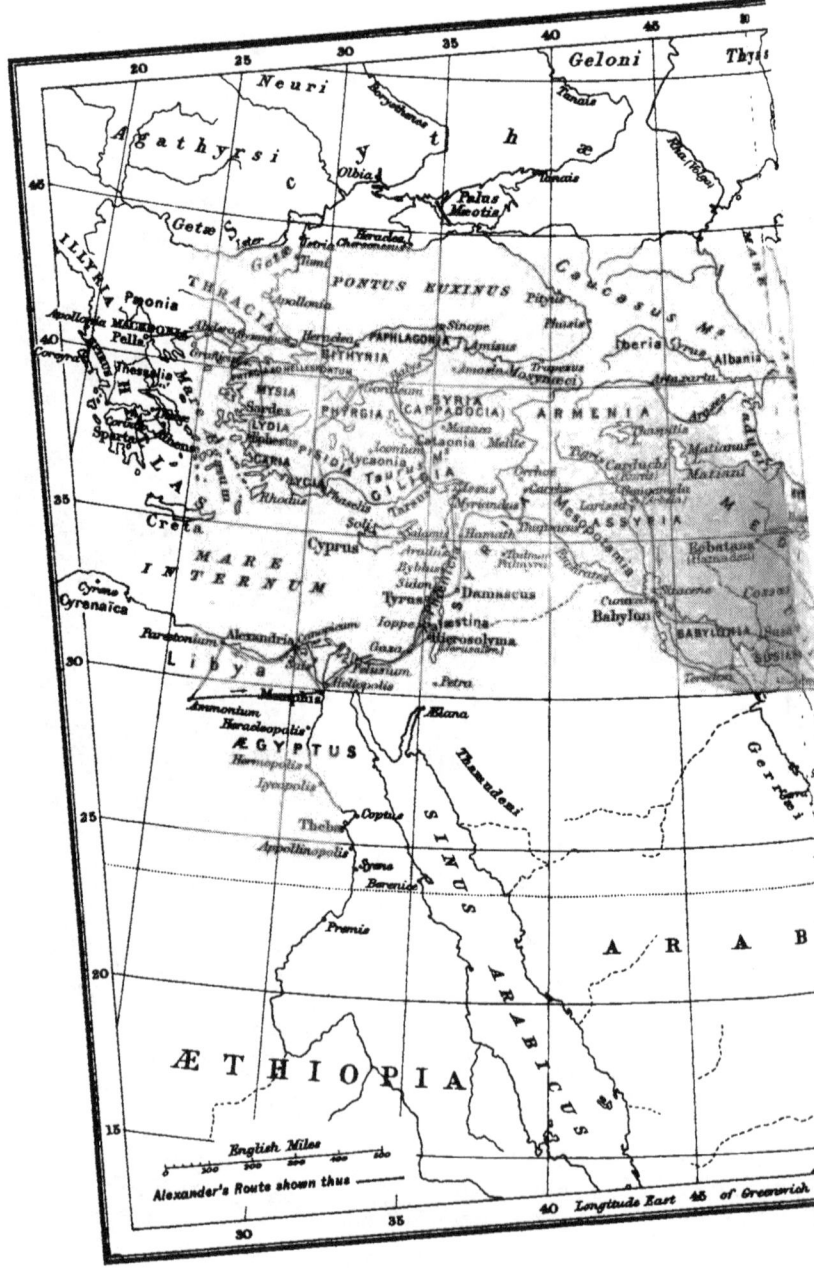

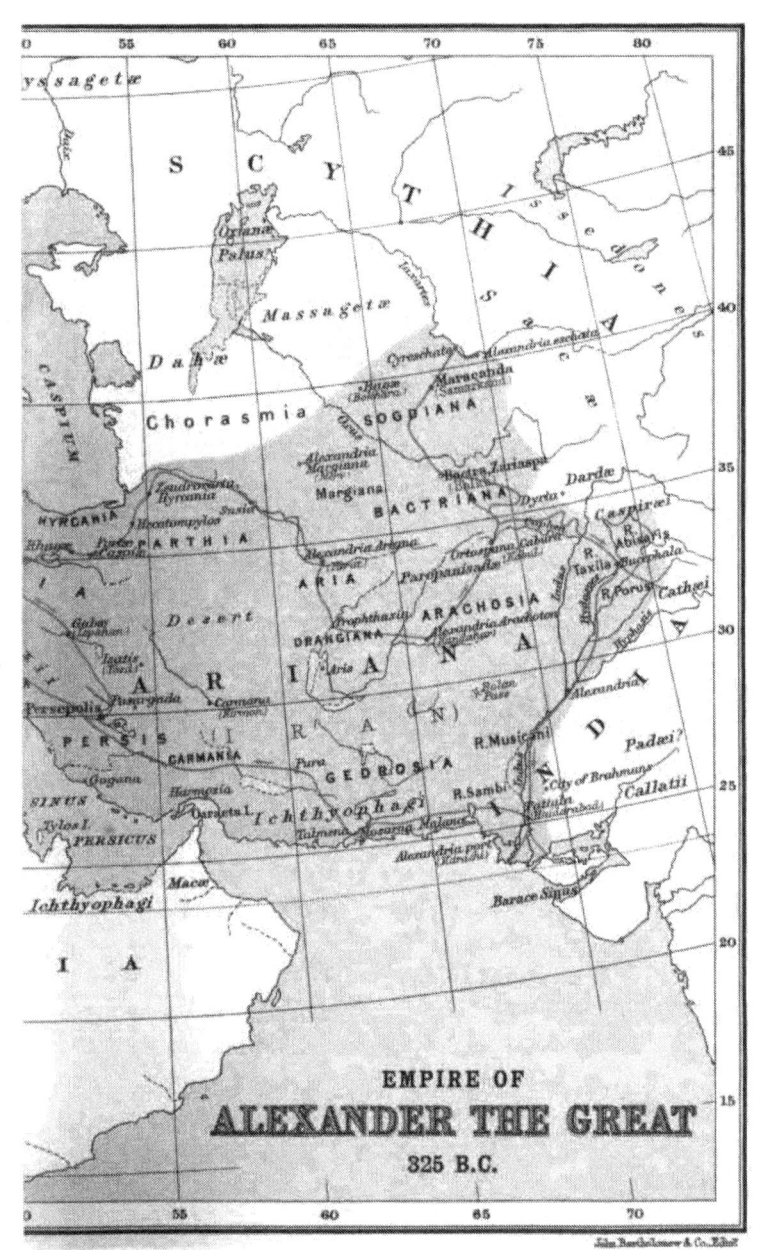

Asia; and sad to say, in his Persian mode of living he forgot some of the teachings of his old master Aristotle. But he was ruler of a great empire only two years when he was attacked by a fever and died at the age of thirty-two (323 B.C.).

Alexander had ruled for twelve years, and in that short time he had become master of nearly all the known world, and to-day he is called in history Alexander the Great.

In his conquest he founded seventy cities and threw open the East to the wisdom and freedom of the Greeks, and it is said that wherever he went he left something better than he found. But he did more than this; he enlarged the map of the world by exploring unknown lands and making India known to the West.

Dying Alexander

After Alexander's death his empire was divided and Ptol'e-my, one of his favorite generals, received Egypt as his share. Its capital, Al'ex-an'dri-a, not only became the world's intellectual center, as Athens had been in the Age of Pericles, but it became the chief commercial center between the East and the West.

The city was laid out in straight parallel streets, one of which extended westward and was two hundred feet wide. It contained magnificent houses, temples, and public buildings, and it was intersected by another street of the same breadth and grandeur.

Ptolemy wrote a history of Alexander the Great and he founded the famous library of more than four hundred thousand manuscripts, which attracted to Alexandria learned men from all parts of the world. His son, Ptolemy II, erected the first lighthouse on the island of Pharos at the mouth of the harbor of Alexandria. It was one of the wonders of the world, and to-day our English word "pharos" means "lighthouse."

Years later (139 B.C.) there lived in Alexandria Clau'di-us Ptol'e-mæ'us, who was a famous geographer, and his geography was a standard text until the fifteenth century. He told of the roundness of the earth. Columbus studied his work and it, no doubt, aided him in his western voyage.

A Grecian Battle with Elephants from India
From a sarcophagus in the Capitol Museum, Rome

CHAPTER IV

ROME AND THE ROMANS

THE Greeks, as we have seen, contributed much to our American civilization; but other ancient peoples did the same, especially the Romans.

THE CITY OF THE SEVEN HILLS

Rome was known as the City of the Seven Hills. It grew in power until it became the seat of an empire, the greatest empire of the ancient world.

Legend tells us that Rome was founded about three hundred years after the fall of Troy. One of the heroes of Troy, who had fought bravely on the losing side, was Æ-ne′as. He was said to be a descendant of Jupiter and a son of the beautiful goddess Venus. Æneas left the ruined city and became a wanderer. After visiting the different countries about the Mediterranean, he settled on the western coast of Italy, near the mouth of the Ti′ber, where he lived with a people called Latins. The King of the Latins had a beautiful daughter, La-vin′ia, who became the wife of the Trojan wanderer. The story of Æneas is told in a long Latin poem called the Æ-ne′id, written by Vir′gil, one of the greatest of the Roman poets. And to-day this poem is read in the high school.

Three hundred years after the coming of Æneas, one of his descendants became the founder of the wonderful City of the Seven Hills, that was destined to rule the world.

This is the well-known story: Rom'u-lus and Remus were twin baby boys, the sons of a king. But a wicked uncle, their father's own brother, seized the throne, making himself king, and threw the twins into the river Tiber.

Romulus and Remus guarded by Shepherds

Romulus and Remus were not drowned, however. They were washed ashore near the foot of the Pal'a-tine, one of the famous seven hills, and found there by a shepherd; the story tells us that a mother-wolf nursed them with her cubs. They grew to be men, handsome and strong, and leaders among the shepherds with whom they lived. One day their aged grandfather, who was still living, recognized them as the long-lost twins. Soon they made war upon their unworthy uncle, slew him, and restored the throne to the rightful king, their father.

Not long after this, in the year 753 B.C., Romulus

founded a city on the Palatine Hill and called it Rome, after his own name. His followers were called Romans. Many of the discontented came from the surrounding country to Rome and helped to build the new city, and it grew very rapidly. Romulus was king for thirty-seven years, when, the legend says, he was carried to the skies, and was afterward worshiped as a Roman god.

Such is the story of the beginning of Rome. We need not believe all of it. No doubt many of the incidents are fanciful. But the Romans believed them for hundreds of years, and perhaps they were in part founded on real happenings. As the story goes (and this portion of it may be true) Rome had seven kings; its people were warlike and fought with their neighbors on all sides, usually winning their battles and extending their territory.

We have noticed that the Romans began their city on the Palatine Hill; but it was not long before they united with a people called Sa'bines, who occupied the Quir'i-nal Hill, and the two became one city. The next hill to be annexed was the Cæ'li-an Hill. And so it continued until all the seven hills were included in the city, and then a great wall was built around it.

HORATIUS AT THE BRIDGE

During the period of the seven kings, nearly 250 years, the Romans were at war most of the time, and many were the stories of heroic deeds of those ancient wars. Let us notice one, the story of Ho-ra'ti-us at the bridge.

The last of the seven kings was Tar'quin. He was a

tyrant. He laid heavy burdens on the people and refused to permit them to assemble for the festivals to which they had been accustomed for many years. At length they rose against him, drove him out of the city, and set up a republic.

Tarquin appealed to the E-trus'cans, a neighboring people who occupied E-tru'ri-a, across the Tiber from Rome. A large army was raised to march upon Rome. It was led by Lars Por'sen-na, prince of Clu'si-um, a city of Etruria.

When the Romans saw the great army, with its thousands of gleaming spears, approaching the Tiber they were dismayed. They had no such army to march against the Etruscan legions. What could be done? There was a wooden bridge across the Tiber and the enemy was rapidly approaching it. If only the bridge could be destroyed, the city might yet be saved. Men were sent to cut it down, but before they could finish the work the enemy came up.

Now rushed forward a young man named Horatius and declared, "If two others will go with me I will go to the farther end of the bridge and keep the enemy at bay till the bridge can be destroyed." As soon as he said this, two young men leaped forward and the brave three were soon at the far end battling like giants with the advance guard of the enemy.

Meanwhile the men with axes were cutting away the bridge, striking blow after blow upon the heavy timbers. Soon the bridge began to totter. The people called to Horatius and his companions to hurry across and save their lives. The two men ran back.

HORATIUS AT THE BRIDGE

But not Horatius; he remained and fought the enemy single-handed. Then came the crash of breaking timbers and the bridge fell into the water below. Horatius then, with a prayer to Father Tiber, leaped into the stream, with his helmet and arms, and swam bravely to the other shore. He was received with wild shouts and cheering, and his name became a household word through all the later history of Rome. Lars Porsenna turned back with his army and the city was saved. Lord Ma-cau'lay wrote a ballad on Horatius at the Bridge. Here are two of the stanzas:

The Dauntless Three

"Hew down the bridge, Sir Consul,
　With all the speed ye may;
I with two more to help me
　Will hold the foe at bay.
In yon straight path a thousand
　May well be stopped by three;
Now who will stand on either hand
　And keep the bridge with me?"

. . . . . .

And still his name sounds stirring
　Unto the men of Rome,
As the trumpet blast that cries to them
　To charge the Volscian home.

> And wives still pray to Juno
> For boys with hearts as bold
> As he who kept the bridge so well
> In the brave days of old.

THE SACRED MOUNT

It was in the year 509 B.C. that the Roman people drove out their last king and set up a republic. "There shall never be another king," they said, and the republic lasted for five hundred years. Instead of a king they elected two consuls, who held their power for one year only. But in time of great danger a dictator was appointed for six months and was given the power of a king.

The Romans, like most peoples, came to be divided into two classes — the rich and the poor. The rich were called pa-tri′cians, and the poor, ple-be′ians. The patricians had control of the government, held all the high offices, and lived within the city. The plebeians were for the most part farmers who lived outside the city walls. They made up the armies and the patricians commanded them. When an enemy approached, the rich man's home was protected by the city walls, but the poor man's farm was overrun, his crops destroyed, and his house burned. Then he had to borrow money from the rich to begin anew.

Were the patricians grateful to the plebeians for protecting the city, and would they lend them money on easy terms? No; on the contrary, they charged high interest and made harsh laws against debtors. If a man could not pay his debts he was thrown into a dungeon or sold, with his family, into slavery.

One day a man in ragged garments, his face showing starvation, ran into the Forum, or market-place. A crowd gathered about him and he told his pitiful story. He had been in many wars in defense of Rome. The armies had destroyed his crops, driven off his cattle, and burned his home. He then borrowed money and the interest was so high that the debt increased. He sold his farm; but still he could not pay all and he was thrown into a dungeon, from which he had just escaped. He bared his body to show the scars he had received in the wars.

The people around him became excited. They cried out against the cruel patricians. The plebeians thereupon decided to leave Rome, and though there was a foreign army approaching, they refused to enlist as soldiers. They crossed the An'i-o, a little stream that flows into the Tiber a few miles from Rome. Here they encamped on a hill, which was ever afterward called Sacred Mount, and they decided to build a city of their own.

The patricians quickly saw that they could not get along without the common people, and they sent messengers to persuade them to come back. The plebeians agreed to return on the condition that all prisoners for debt be released and that henceforth they should have officers of their own who could veto or cancel unjust laws. The patricians consented to this and the two parties were reconciled. These officers of the plebeians were called Tribunes of the People. This was the first step made by the people in gaining power in the government of Rome.

The story of the plebeians and Sacred Mount may be founded in fact, but it belongs to the age of legend, as does also the following story of Cin-cin-na′tus.

CINCINNATUS

About fifty years after the founding of the republic the Romans were at war with the Æ′qui-ans, who had a large army in a field near Alba Longa, which is not far from Rome. A Roman army was sent against them, but it was defeated and almost surrounded by the enemy. Five men escaped and hurried to Rome with the dreadful news. What could be done? If the Roman army were destroyed the city would be at the mercy of the invaders.

On the banks of the Tiber there lived a farmer named Cincinnatus, and the eyes of all turned to him as the deliverer of the city. Why, we do not know. Perhaps he had been a conqueror in former wars; but the legend does not say. Messengers were sent to tell him of the peril of the city and that he had been appointed dictator.

Cincinnatus was in his field plowing when the messengers came. He accepted the great trust and hurried to Rome to raise an army. He ordered all private business to stop and commanded every man that could bear arms to join him. Within a day or two he was marching with a large army in the direction of Alba Longa. He met the Æquians, defeated them, and captured their entire army. He then forced the captured army to pass under the yoke. This was made of three spears — two fastened upright in the ground and a third across them at the top. Each captured soldier had to creep under this yoke to show that he was subdued. And to-day we have the English word "subjugation," from two Latin words which mean "under the yoke."

Cincinnatus receiving the Dictatorship

The Roman people were wild with joy at the victory and they showered their blessings on the man who had saved them. Sixteen days after Cincinnatus had left his plow he had laid aside his great power and was again back on his farm. He had saved the city, and his name, like the name of Horatius, became a household word in Rome.

George Washington has been called the Cincinnatus of the West. After our Revolutionary War was over a company of officers was formed and called the Cincinnati, and a newly founded city in Ohio was given the same name.

THE FIRST PUNIC WAR AND REGULUS

For four hundred years after the founding of Rome there was almost constant war between that city and the various nations that occupied Italy. Some of these wars were fierce and bloody and the Romans were often defeated, but in the end they won everywhere, and all Italy came under Roman government.

But this is not the whole story. After becoming master of Italy, Rome extended her conquests to all the countries bordering on the Mediterranean. There were North Africa, Spain and France, Mac′e-do′ni-a and Greece, Asia Minor, Pal′es-tine, and even England — all of which became parts of the mighty Roman Empire. Let us notice here one of these conquests, that which came through the Pu′nic wars.

Roman Column in honor of first naval Victory over Carthage

Punic means Carth′a-gin′i-an, and these wars were with Car′thage, a city of North Africa. Carthage had been founded by the Phœ-ni′cians about a hundred years before the founding of Rome. It was a great city; it governed the island of Sar-din′i-a, a large part of Sic′i-ly, and the coast of North Africa for a thousand miles; it had a prosperous trade with the countries

THE FIRST PUNIC WAR AND REGULUS

around the Mediterranean and it had even sent ships through the Strait of Gi-bral'tar.

It was not long before Rome and Carthage came into conflict. Each was jealous of the growing power of the other and the mastery of the Mediterranean was determined in a series of wars that covered more than a hundred years.

The first of the Punic wars began in 264 B.C. and continued twenty-four years. In one respect Carthage had a great advantage over Rome. She had powerful ships and a large number of them. Rome had no navy and she clearly saw that without one she could not hope for success against her great rival. The Romans thereupon set to work building a navy. Taking as a model an old Carthaginian vessel wrecked on the Italian shore, they worked day and night, and in sixty days, it is said, had finished a hundred warships. These were not such war vessels as we now have; but they were very good for those days, and from this time on Rome was able to meet her great enemy on the sea as well as on the land.

The most famous story of the First Punic War was that about Reg'u-lus. The Romans carried the war into Africa and sent Regulus with an army to that country. The army was defeated and Regulus taken prisoner. The Carthaginians desired peace and they sent Regulus back to Rome on his promise that, if he did not succeed in making terms of peace, he would return to Carthage. He went to Rome, and instead of trying to make peace, he urged the Romans to continue the war. They did, and Regulus returned to

Carthage, as he had promised to do, and it is said that he was put to death.

THE SECOND PUNIC WAR AND HANNIBAL

The story of the Second Punic War centers around one great man — Hannibal. He was the son of a great Carthaginian commander named Ha-mil'car, who had fought in the First Punic War.

When Hannibal was a boy of nine years his father had him take a most solemn oath that he would spend his life fighting Rome. A little later the father was killed in a battle in Spain, and as the boy grew to manhood he prepared to fulfil the oath, and later he proved himself the greatest commander of ancient times.

Hannibal

While still a young man he started out on his life-work. He raised a great army and led it from Spain to Italy by land, across the Pyr'e-nees and the Alps. This was in the year 218 B.C. Five months after leaving Spain Hannibal swept down into northern Italy. The Romans sent an army against him, but he defeated it with great slaughter in the battle of Tre'bi-a. Again, at Lake Tras-i-me'ne, Hannibal won a great victory over the Roman hosts and there was dismay in the City of the Seven Hills. The people feared that the great Carthaginian would capture the city and perhaps destroy it.

At length the Romans found a general who was wise enough to meet the enemy. His name was Fa'bi-us. Being made dictator with unlimited power, he led an army toward the invader. But Fabius avoided a battle because he knew that his army could not stand before his great enemy. He encamped on the hill, where Hannibal's cavalry could not reach him. Hannibal tried in every way to draw the Roman general into battle, but he did not succeed. Fabius followed his enemy wherever he went, cut off his food supply, and annoyed him wherever he could, but remained just out of reach.

Hannibal grew very tired of such tactics. He desired to fight and not to see his army wasted away with such annoyance. At length he played a trick on Fabius that proved successful.

The Roman people became very impatient of their general. They could not understand why he would not fight the enemy. They even accused him of being a traitor to his country and on friendly terms with Hannibal. At this time Hannibal, who knew of the suspicion against Fabius, passed through a country where Fabius had a fine estate — a grand mansion, a beautiful garden, and broad lands. Now the trick Hannibal played was this: he laid waste all the country round, except the lands of Fabius. He set guards around the property and would not permit a soldier to destroy anything.

What was the result? The Romans now cried out fiercely against Fabius. Here was the proof, they said, that he was false to his country and that Hannibal was his friend. Fabius was recalled — just what Hannibal desired.

The next year an officer named Var'ro commanded the Romans. Then came the greatest battle of the war and the greatest disaster that ever befell a Roman army. It was the battle of Can'næ. It took place near the Au'fi-dus River, in 216 B.C. Varro had a Roman army of eighty thousand men, the flower of all Italy. He would not follow the tactics of Fabius. No, he came out to fight and proposed to do so.

Hannibal saw his opportunity. He placed his weakest soldiers in the center and his strongest, with the cavalry, on the flanks or wings. Varro rushed in with his whole force and struck at the Carthaginian center. It was soon pressed back, as Hannibal knew it would be, and his army was in the shape of a half-moon, the Romans filling the concave. The Carthaginians then closed in from both wings and almost surrounded the Roman army.

Then began the most dreadful slaughter. The Carthaginian horsemen cut down the Romans by thousands. At the close of that bloody day fifty thousand of Varro's forces lay dead or wounded on the field. Twenty thousand were captured and barely ten thousand escaped to return to their homes.

The people, after this awful day at Cannæ, began to see that Fabius was their true commander. They realized that Hannibal was too skilful to be defeated in open battle. He remained many years longer in Italy, but never fought a great battle after Cannæ. Fabius was restored to public favor and to this day his name stands among the great in Roman history.

Hannibal was fifteen years on the soil of Italy. But the Romans at last found a way to get rid of him. They sent a large army to Africa to threaten Carthage. It was led by a strong young commander named Scip′i-o. The men of Carthage had no commander strong enough to meet Scipio and they called for Hannibal to come home. He returned and raised an army against the Romans. But his forces were inferior and he was defeated in the great battle of Za′ma, in the year 202 B.C.

Thus ended the Second Punic War, and Rome was the victor. Hannibal did all he could to build up the broken fortunes of his country; but a few years later, when the Romans demanded that he be sent to them, he left his native land and became a wanderer. For some years he traveled from one country to another, and at last, fearing that he would fall into the hands of his great enemy, he killed himself. Thus perished one of the greatest commanders in history.

Scipio Africanus

Scipio, after his great victory at Zama, was called Scipio Af-ri-ca′nus. He enjoyed a great triumph when he returned to Rome. A Roman triumph was marching through the streets with great pomp, exhibiting the spoils of war, amid the shouts and applause of the people.

The Third Punic War came about a half century after the Second, and resulted in the utter destruction of the city of Carthage. It is said that the Roman senator Ca'to closed all his speeches in the Senate, on whatever subject, with the words, "Carthage must be destroyed."

At length the Roman armies came and laid siege to the doomed city. For three years the Carthaginians fought with the bravery of despair; but they had to yield at last and their beautiful city was totally destroyed. Not a building was left standing; the people who were not slain were driven away or sold into slavery, fifty thousand being carried to the slave markets of Rome, and the spot on which Carthage stood became a scene of ruin. This occurred in the year 146 B.C.

CORNELIA'S JEWELS

The many wars of the Roman people resulted in greatly changing their mode of living. The simple life of the old days of Horatius and Cincinnatus had passed away. The wars had made some very rich and others very poor. The rich absorbed the little farms of the poor and extended their estates over vast tracts; they built fine houses and laid out beautiful gardens and had broad pasture and hunting lands.

If the rich landowners had employed the poor on their great estates, conditions would not have been so bad; but they did not. They had all their work done by slaves, chiefly men captured in the wars. There were hundreds, sometimes thousands, of slaves on a single estate. During the day they worked in the fields, chained in gangs and driven by a taskmaster. At night they were locked in a dungeon. But after all, the slave had a place to stay and enough to eat.

Not so with the poor farmers. They had lost

Cornelia, Mother of the Gracchi
From the painting by J. Jarnelo

their homes, often through fighting for their country, and they had no place to go and no way of making a living. Many of them flocked to the city and became paupers. There were no large factories, as in modern cities, to furnish employment for laborers. Others wandered about the country with their wives and children and obtained a living as best they could.

84   THE STORY OF THE OLD WORLD

The greedy landowners who had taken their farms cared nothing about their sufferings. Now we come to the story of Cor-ne′lia and her jewels.

Cornelia was the daughter of Scipio, the great general who had defeated Hannibal at Zama. She was of a noble family, but she married a man of the common people whose name was Grac′chus. He was a person of high character and honor. But it was not many years before Gracchus died and Cornelia was left a widow with two little boys.

She was still young and beautiful and several prominent men, one of whom was a king, sought her hand in marriage. But she decided that she would not marry again and that she would devote her time to training her two boys. The name of the elder was Ti-be′ri-us, and the younger, Ca′ius. Later they were called the Grac′chi, as the word Gracchi is the plural of Gracchus.

One day some rich matrons of Rome were visiting Cornelia and were displaying their jewels — golden ornaments and precious stones. "Where are your jewels?" asked one of the women. The proud mother pointed to her two little boys and answered, "These are my jewels."

The brothers grew to manhood and were known for their nobleness of character. Tiberius, the elder brother, served in the wars of Africa and Spain. As he passed through the districts outside of Rome his heart was moved with pity at the great numbers of poor farmers wandering aimlessly, having been driven from their homes by the rich landowners.

Tiberius was so stirred by these conditions, that

when he returned from the war he began an attack against the Roman land system. "The poor have fought to maintain the luxury of the rich," he said, "while they do not possess a clod of earth that they may call their own." He told the people that the wild beasts had their dens and caves, but the men who had offered their lives for their country had to wander about homeless with their wives and little ones.

There was an ancient law, two hundred years old, which forbade anyone to own a large estate; but this law was disregarded by the rich and it was not enforced. Tiberius set about to revive this law. Cornelia urged her sons to do something great for their country. "I am known," she said, "as the daughter of Scipio, but I wish to be remembered as the mother of the Gracchi."

The opportunity soon came. Tiberius was elected Tribune of the people, and he declared that the old law in regard to the division of the land should be revived or a new one passed. But the senators, most of whom were holders of large estates, objected. Tiberius made a noble fight and won a victory. The law was passed and three commissioners appointed to carry it into effect. Tiberius, however, made many bitter enemies among the rich, and a little later, on election day, when he was a candidate for a second term, a great riot occurred. The streets of Rome flowed with blood. About three hundred people were killed and among the dead was the noble reformer Tiberius.

When he was slain the people were without a leader. His brother Caius was in Spain. On his return he saw that the laws of his dead brother were not properly carried out; the people were wandering about like sheep without a shepherd, and he became their leader.

Caius was the most eloquent man in Rome. Great crowds gathered to hear him speak in the Forum and thousands were won by his voice as he pleaded the cause of the downtrodden poor. Like his brother he was elected Tribune (123 B.C.) and he brought about some good laws, such as the law to sell corn to the poor from the public stores at a very low price. He restored the land laws of Tiberius and sought to build colonies of the poor outside the city.

Caius Gracchus

But he was hated by the rich, as his brother had been. At length his enemies made an attack and three thousand people were slain. Caius fled across the Tiber and there, rather than fall into the hands of his enemies alive, he ordered a faithful slave to kill him with the sword. The slave did as he was commanded and then he slew himself. Thus perished the second of the noble sons of a noble mother.

Some of the laws of the Gracchi continued in force; but for the most part Rome was governed by the rich and the poor were severely oppressed. As long as she lived the mother of Tiberius and Caius mourned the death of her brave sons; and while she was still living a statue of her was set up in Rome and on it was this inscription: "Cornelia, the Mother of the Gracchi."

CHAPTER V

Cæsar and the West

Marcus Tullius Cicero
Bust in Vatican Museum

THE greatest of all the Romans that ever lived was Ju'lius Cæ'sar, and his name is perhaps the most famous in history. Born in the year 100 B.C., descended from a noble family, Cæsar entered public life at an early age and rose from one position to another until he became master of Rome, and that meant master of the world.

EARLY LIFE OF CAESAR

As a youth Cæsar was gay and thoughtless and a leader of fashion among the young nobles. He gave little promise of future greatness. But now and then he showed the metal of which he was made. At one time he was captured by the pirates of the Mediterranean, who held him for ransom. They demanded twenty talents for his release. A talent was worth more than a thousand dollars. Cæsar scornfully told the pirates that they did not know the value of their captive, and that he would pay them fifty talents. His friends paid the ransom a few months later. During the time that Cæsar was with the pirates he entered into their games and made himself agreeable; but he told them that the time would come when he would capture and hang them. And he kept his word.

It is said that at one time, when Cæsar was about thirty years of age, he stood before a statue of Alexander the Great, and he burst into tears, saying again and again, "At my age he had conquered the world, and as yet I have done nothing." Let us now take a view of the wonderful career of this Roman.

Caius Julius Cæsar
National Museum, Naples

For many years after the death of Caius Gracchus the rich governed the country and the poor were trampled in the dust. From time to time leaders arose, but they thought more of their own selfish interests than of the welfare of their country and there was great disorder in Rome. Among the leaders were Mar'i-us and Sul'la, both great commanders, who fought each other until the government was almost ruined.

At length there were three men who gained control of the government, and they were called the Triumvirate, which means "the three men." They were Pom'pey, a famous warrior known as Pompey the

Great; Cras'sus, a man of boundless wealth; and
Cæsar, who was very popular with the masses. Cæsar
was soon afterward elected consul, and he had a law
passed to distribute public lands among the poor,
similar to the law of Tiberius. The senate, composed
of rich men and nobles, bitterly opposed Cæsar and
looked with alarm on his growing popularity. He had
kept every promise made to the people and had won
in every contest with his enemies.

At the close of his consulship Cæsar became governor
of Gaul for a term of five years. What was then called
Gaul is now France. It included also what is now
Switzerland and Belgium.

Over all this vast province Cæsar had full control,
and here at last was his opportunity to show his great
power as a commander of armies. He had won a few
victories in Spain, but his new province was far more
difficult to subdue. The Gauls were divided into many
warlike tribes. They had been for centuries a terror
to Rome. At one time they had captured and burned
the City of the Seven Hills and never had the Romans
been able to conquer them.

TWO GREAT ROMANS

Before following Cæsar into Gaul let us notice two
other statesmen of this time. One was Cic'er-o, the
famous orator, and the other was Ca'to, who was
noted for honesty in public life in an age when few
honest men could be found. Cato was a great-grandson
of that Cato who always closed his speeches in the
senate with the words, "Carthage must be destroyed."

The younger Cato was a friend of Cicero and both were among the best men of their time. One day, as Cato was walking in a public park with a friend admiring the statues of public men, the friend said to him, "Cato, why is not your statue here among the rest?" And he answered, "I had rather hear you ask that question than hear someone ask, Why is it here?"

The greatest service Cicero rendered his country was when he exposed a band of conspirators led by an evil man named Cat'i-line. Cicero was consul when he discovered the plot. It was in the year 63 B.C., the same year in which Pompey captured Jerusalem, the holy city of the Jews, and made Palestine a Roman province.

Catiline had a great many followers among the wicked men. Their intention was to assassinate the consuls and many other public officers, to set fire to the city of Rome in a hundred places, and to overturn the government. Cicero had a secret way of finding out the entire working of the plot, and in several powerful speeches in the senate he exposed the whole scheme. These speeches are known as Cicero's Orations and they are still read in our schools.

Catiline, who was a senator, sat and listened to Cicero's fearful charges against him. At length he rose and rushed from the senate chamber. That night he fled from the city and joined his armed forces across the Tiber. He left instructions with his fellow conspirators in the city to assassinate Cicero if possible and to be ready to apply the torch to Rome as soon as he should appear before the walls of the city with his troops. But Cicero had spies watching every movement the plotters made, and it was not long before several of them were arrested and put to death as public enemies. Catiline perished a little later at the head of his troops fighting against a Roman army.

Cicero had done a noble service for his country. No doubt he saved the city from a dreadful calamity. Cato hailed him with the title "Father of his Country." But a few years later, when one of his enemies came into power, Cicero was banished from Rome because, it was said, he had put the conspirators to death in an unlawful way. However, after sixteen months in exile he was recalled, and as he was returning to Rome crowds of people greeted him with cheers and shouts of welcome. Cicero's later years were spent chiefly in writing books, which still exist, and are among the finest specimens of literature that have come to us from the ancient world.

CÆSAR AND THE GAULS

In the year 58 B.C. Cæsar with an army entered the province of Gaul and for six or seven years he waged war upon the inhabitants. Cæsar had more than one object in conquering the Gauls; he wished to reduce the country to a Roman province, and, it must be added, he wished to make a great name for himself and to become the leading man in Rome. In both he was successful. He wrote a history of his campaigns in Gaul. This is called "Cæsar's Commentaries," and it is one of the first Latin books read in our high schools.

Cæsar had wonderful power in attaching his soldiers to him. He was dignified, but he was gracious and never cruel. At his command his men were ready to face death anywhere, so devoted were they. And even the Gauls whom he conquered, many of them, were won to his standard. He bestowed offices on the leaders and induced many of the soldiers to join his own army.

Among the first of the results of this war with Gaul was the turning back of the Hel-ve′tians. These people lived among the Swiss Alps, and being oppressed by their neighbors, they decided to migrate in a body to western Gaul, perhaps to the shore of the great ocean of which they had heard. It was not unusual in those days for whole nations or tribes to move from one country to another.

A captive Gaul

Cæsar gives the number of Helvetians as 368,000, nearly a hundred thousand of whom were men bearing arms. Having burned their towns, villages, and homes, they set out. Cæsar met them on the banks of the Rhone River, near Lake Geneva, and told them they must turn back. They refused and war followed. More than two-thirds of the Helvetians were slain or lost and the remainder returned to the ruined homes which they had left.

Soon after these events the Roman general had a similar experience with the Germans. Great numbers of them, led by Ar-i-o-vis′tus, were swarming across the Rhine into northern Gaul. The people in this part of Gaul were friendly to the Romans and they appealed to Cæsar for protection from the barbarians. Cæsar called on Ariovistus to cease bringing over his tribes, but the German king made a bold answer. "My warriors have never been beaten," he declared, and he added that they were thoroughly trained and had not slept under a roof for fourteen years.

Now occurred almost a panic in the Roman army. Officers and men were filled with fear at the thought of entering the dark German forests and of fighting with the fierce, unconquered tribes of barbarians. Cæsar called a great council of war, and he addressed its members. His words inspired his army with his own undaunted courage. The cheers of his troops at the close of his speech assured him that there would be no further hesitation.

Soon after this a terrible battle was fought between Cæsar and Ariovistus, resulting in a great victory for the Romans. The German king, with the remnant of his army, escaped across the Rhine, and the invasions of Gaul for the time were at an end.

But the Gauls had no sooner been delivered from the Germans than they became tired of the Romans and rose against them. Cæsar therefore spent several years in almost constant warfare. In 55 B.C. he made an invasion of Britain, but remained only a few weeks. The next year he again made a voyage to Britain, remaining several months and winning a few slight battles. On the promise of tribute he returned to the continent; but the tribute was probably never paid,

Return of the Germans after Battle

Redrawn from the painting by Thumann

and more than a hundred years passed before Britain became in fact a Roman possession.

In his Gallic wars Cæsar displayed wonderful skill as a commander, but now and then he had serious drawbacks. At one time one of his legions was destroyed, and another, under the command of Quintus Cicero, a brother of the great Roman orator, was penned up in a town with sixty thousand armed Gauls surrounding it. Cæsar, who was far away, hearing of the condition of Cicero and his army, sent a horseman with a despatch. It was written in Greek, so that the enemy could not read it, should it fall into their hands. The messenger was instructed to fasten the paper to a javelin and shoot it into the camp. This he did, but the javelin struck into a tower and was not noticed for two days. When at length it was found it was brought to Cicero. He read it — only three words: "Courage, help approaches."

This gave the men renewed courage. A few days later Cæsar arrived and rescued the besieged men. Nine out of every ten of them had been killed or wounded.

THE STORY OF VERCINGETORIX

The greatest leader that ever rose among the early Gauls was Ver'cin-get'o-rix. What his real name was we do not know. The long name by which he is known must have been given him after he became a famous warrior, for the word means "The Great Chief of the Brave."

After Cæsar had been in Gaul for six years and had the whole country under his control, he was astonished to learn that great numbers of the Gauls had risen against the Romans. Their leader was Vercingetorix, a man tall and strong, with a proud, soldier-like bearing, and with long, flowing light hair. He believed that the Gauls should be independent of the Romans and he offered to lead them in a war for independence. He called on the tribes from the Alps to the sea to rally

German Bodyguard of a Roman Emperor
Detail from column of Trajan

in a mighty effort to throw off the Roman yoke. The men came in uncounted thousands.

Cæsar hastened to gather his army and begin a new campaign against the Gauls. He found in their leader the ablest foe he had ever met in battle. But as the Roman army was so much better trained they won in most of the contests though there were heavy losses on both sides.

At last the brave Gallic commander found refuge in the town of A-le′si-a, situated on the flat top of a steep hill. It was one of the strongest fortresses in Gaul. But Cæsar's army soon surrounded the city and began a siege. He dug a deep ditch and built a high rampart.

Meantime a great army of Gauls gathered from the country round and attacked the Romans in the rear. But they had no strong commander and the Romans defeated them.

Finally there was a terrible battle in which the Gauls attacked the Romans from within the city and from without. Again the Romans were successful and the Gauls were utterly defeated.

Vercingetorix saw that all was lost. This brave and noble man had one more duty to perform. He would sacrifice himself to save his people. Knowing that the city could hold out no longer, he said to his officers, "I did not undertake this war to raise my fortune, but to save the common liberty. Put me to death to satisfy the Romans, or give me up alive."

A little later the gates of the town were opened. A lone horseman rode forth on a splendid war steed. He wore his rich and shining armor. Galloping up to the tribunal where Cæsar sat he circled round it, then leaped from his horse and without uttering a word, but with a proud, unconquered look, he cast his helmet and his sword at the feet of the great Roman commander. It was Vercingetorix. He thus offered his life for the people in whose behalf he had fought. For six years he was kept in captivity, when he adorned a triumph through the streets of Rome, after which he was cruelly put to death.

After one more campaign in the northeast Gaul was completely conquered at last and Cæsar was hailed as the greatest commander in the world. What will be the next scene in the great Roman drama?

CROSSING THE RUBICON

The Ru'bi-con is a very small river in northeastern Italy flowing into the A'dri-at'ic Sea. But it became famous in history.

We have noticed that three men — Cæsar, Pom'pey, and Crassus — formed a triumvirate and governed Rome. But Crassus went to the East to fight the Par'thi-ans and was slain. Cæsar went into Gaul, as we have seen, and as the fame of his conquests reached Rome the people were loud in their praise. Pompey became jealous, and so did the members of the senate.

German horsemen fighting Cæsar's legions
Detail from column of Antonius

Cæsar was certainly a wonderful man. He was of medium size, had a pale complexion, and he was not robust in health. Many supposed that a hard campaign or two would end his career. But they were astonished at the reports of his actions amid the forests and mountains of the North. Often he fared no better than his men. He swam rapid rivers and climbed rugged mountains in midwinter. He shared the hardships of camp life with his soldiers. He knew the smallest details about his army and could call thousands of his men by name. He often dictated four or five letters at a time to as many secretaries.

For many years Pompey had been considered the greatest man in Rome. At one time he boasted that he could stamp his foot and fill all Italy with armed soldiers. But now it was clear that the fame of Cæsar was eclipsing his own, and Pompey was greatly disturbed. Cæsar had been appointed ruler of Gaul for a second term of five years. This was now about to expire and he expected to be chosen consul when he returned to Rome. His territory extended to the Rubicon River, but south of it he dared not come without the consent of the senate. The senate called on him to disband his army before returning to Rome. Cæsar answered that he would if Pompey would disband his, but the latter refused.

Now there was trouble for Cæsar. He had carried the Roman Eagles to the far North and had deserved the gratitude of the nation. The people and his army were devoted to him, but the senate was filled with his enemies, who were seeking to destroy him, and he knew that if he entered the city without an army to protect him he would fall into their hands. One senator had said that he should be arrested as soon as he became a private citizen. At length the senate declared, "If Cæsar does not dismiss his army by a certain time he shall be considered an enemy to the state."

But two ways were left to Cæsar — to give himself into the hands of his enemies, or to cross the Rubicon and march with his army upon Rome. It is said that he hesitated long; that he consulted his army and they declared that they would follow wherever he chose to lead them. He decided to march upon Rome (49 B.C.), but on reaching the boundary line, the little Rubicon, again he hesitated. But at length he plunged his horse into the stream, exclaiming, "The die is cast," and Cæsar marched upon the seven-hilled city, unbidden, with his army. Since then, when some great decision is to be made, it is called crossing the Rubicon.

As Cæsar approached there was reason for confusion in Rome. Pompey did not feel able to meet this great general and he fled from the city and escaped to Greece. Many of the senators and their friends fled also, and Cæsar found himself master of Rome and all Italy, almost without bloodshed.

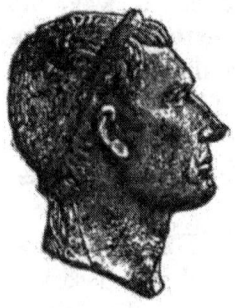

Julius Cæsar

After making an excursion into Spain and defeating an army of Pompey stationed there, Cæsar returned and went to Greece in pursuit of the enemy himself. At the battle of Phar-sa'lus Pompey was defeated and he fled to Egypt, where he was murdered on landing, by order of King Ptol'e-my, who expected by this act to win the favor of Cæsar. Thus perished the second greatest commander that Rome ever produced.

When Cæsar reached Egypt and heard of the death of Pompey, it is said that he burst into tears. Ptolemy had failed to win the favor of the Roman commander, and as there was a dispute between Ptolemy and his sister Cle'o-pa'tra as to which should occupy the Egyptian throne, Cæsar decided for Cleopatra, and placing her on the throne, protected her with Roman legions.

Returning to Italy by way of Asia Minor, Cæsar

put down a revolt in Pontus and described his victory in three famous words, "Veni, vidi, vici" (I came, I saw, I conquered). After another successful campaign in Africa and one in Spain, Julius Cæsar stood forth the undisputed master of the Roman world with all its vast possessions — Greece and Asia Minor, Palestine, Gaul, Spain, North Africa, and the islands of the sea. What will he do with his great power?

LAST YEARS AND DEATH OF CAESAR

The greatest honors were heaped on Cæsar after his final victories. He was made dictator for ten years, with almost the power of an absolute monarch. Four triumphs were celebrated in honor of his victories and forty days of thanksgiving were decreed by the new senate. Temples and statues were dedicated in his honor and one of the months was renamed July, after his name Julius.

The burning question among Cæsar's former enemies was, How will he treat us? Other conquerors had destroyed their enemies after peace was restored. But Cæsar had no revenge in his heart. He gave office to men who had fought against him in Pompey's army. In his triumphs, when conquered enemies were led captive through the streets, not a Roman citizen was among them. On the other hand, Cæsar gave a great feast to the people, using twenty-two thousand tables. Many who had fought against him were among the guests. He furnished games in which there were wrestling and dancing and chariot races. Four hundred lions were slain in the arena of the amphitheater to entertain the multitudes. Cæsar pardoned those who had fought against him. He had been severe in war, but he was kind and generous in peace.

For a hundred years the government of Rome had been in the hands of a few warring factions. When Cæsar came into power he set about making the government better and breaking down the barrier between the rich and the poor. Many thousands of the Roman poor he sent out to the provinces, furnishing them with small farms on which they could earn a living.

Before this time the governors of the provinces had robbed the people to enrich themselves. Cæsar changed the system and put a decided check on the practise of robbing the people. He reformed the calendar and it has since remained, with little change, as he left it. Many other things this great ruler planned to do for the welfare of his country, but he did not live to carry them out.

His enemies formed a conspiracy to kill him. More than fifty men were in the plot, and many of them he believed to be his friends. Some of them were opposed to Cæsar because they were jealous of his great power; others sincerely believed that they were doing the state a service by preventing it from becoming a monarchy. The leader of the conspirators was Cas'-si-us, who had been a commander in the army of Crassus. Cassius won over Brutus, one of Cæsar's best friends, who believed that the liberties of the people were in danger.

It was the Ides of March (March 15th) in the year 44 B.C. Cæsar had been warned that there was danger, but he would take no heed. When he entered the senate chamber the conspirators surrounded him and began to strike him with their daggers. At first he tried to defend himself; but when he saw Brutus among the assassins, with upraised knife, he cried bitterly, "And you, Brutus! Then falls Cæsar." And he threw his mantle over his head and fell dead, with twenty-three gushing wounds, at the foot of Pompey's statue.

Brutus

Great was the confusion in Rome when the murder of Cæsar became known. Soon there was civil war, and most of the conspirators lost their lives. Those who expected to save the republic by killing Cæsar were sadly mistaken. It was more than five hundred years since the kings had been driven out and Rome had become a republic; but soon after the death of Cæsar the republic was at an end, and from this time Rome was an empire.

THE EMPIRE AND THE CITY

Julius Cæsar had made Rome a monarchy by gathering up the powers of government into his own hands. But it was not called a monarchy for about fifteen years after his death. The first ruler to be called emperor was Oc-ta'vi-us Cæsar, or Au-gus'tus, as he came to be called. He was a grandnephew of Julius Cæsar. From the time of Augustus, Rome was an empire for nearly five hundred years, when the empire fell to pieces and was no more.

The empire, at the end of the reign of Augustus, extended from the Rhine and the Dan'- ube rivers on the north to the Sa-ha'ra Desert on the south, and from the Atlantic Ocean almost to the Eu-phra'- tes River.

Augustus

Let us take a nearer view of this wonderful city that "sat on her seven hills and ruled the world"; but we can mention only a few of the many interesting points.

One of the seven famous hills of Rome was the Cap'i-to-line, near a bend in the Tiber. On one of its two summits was built the temple of Jupiter and on the other the citadel. The temple was built by the Tarquin kings and for more than four centuries it was the most sacred building in Rome. In 83 B.C. it was set afire by some unknown person. The temple was soon rebuilt and several times during the following centuries it was destroyed and rebuilt. Once a year the people held a great festival and marched up the hill to the temple. A priest then drove a nail into the wall, and thus the record of the years was kept.

This temple was called the Capitol, from the Latin word *caput*, which means "the head." In a chest in the Capitol were kept the three mysterious manuscripts known as the sib'yl-line books. A prophetess, or sibyl, who lived in a cave, came to one of the Roman kings and offered him nine books containing, as she said, prophecies about Rome. But her price was so high that he refused to buy. She departed and burned three of the books. Returning to the king, she offered him the six remaining books for the same price that she had asked for the nine.

Again the king sent her away, and still again she came. This time she had but three books, and she asked the same for the three that she had at first asked for nine. The king hesitated no longer. He purchased the three books. They were placed in a stone chest and guarded day and night. None but the priests were permitted to look into them.

One of the most interesting spots in Rome was the Forum. This was at first a marshy valley nearly enclosed by three of the seven hills — the Capitoline, the Palatine, and the Es'qui-line. It was here that Romulus and the king of the Sabines met and made peace between the two peoples. For many years the Forum was a market-place where the people met to buy and sell their wares and to talk over the latest news. At length the butchers' stalls gave place to grand and stately buildings and beautiful statues.

The most interesting thing perhaps in connection with the Forum was the temple of Vesta. Vesta was the goddess of the hearth and home, and from her name we have the word "vestibule." In the temple were six young women who kept burning the sacred fire day and night for years and even for centuries. They were called the Vestal Virgins.

Vergil reading to Augustus
From painting by Jalabut

In architecture the ideas of the Romans were at first very crude; but in the course of centuries they learned a great deal from their neighbors, especially from the E-trus'cans, who dwelt on the other side of the Tiber, and from the Greeks.

Once in five years the people assembled on the Campus Mar'tius (the plain of Mars), a large open valley outside the city, lying between the hills and the Tiber. Here the census was taken and a sacrifice of a pig, a sheep, and an ox was made for the purification of the people. The Campus Martius was also used for the marshaling of armies, and sometimes the display was magnificent indeed.

The Romans loved entertainment. They had great amphitheaters which would accommodate many thousands of people. In these they gathered in vast numbers to see the shows, and their shows too often were not of a refining nature. Not only were animals slain for the amusement of the people, but human beings also. The men who fought were called gladiators, from *gladius*, a sword. These gladiators were thoroughly trained in the use of the sword. They met one another in the open arena of the amphitheater and fought to the death, the great crowds looking on.

The greatest of the Roman amphitheaters was known as the Col'os-se'um. This was erected at a later date than that which we are here describing. It was built to seat fifty thousand people, with standing room for twenty thousand more. Its structure was of stone, with seats of marble. Its walls were 157 feet in height.

THE COMING OF CHRISTIANITY

The Roman people excelled in war and in government, and thus they became the conquerors of other nations. But they were at first a coarse and crude people, and as time passed they made conquests of peoples who were more cultivated and refined than themselves. The Greeks were far ahead of the Romans in art, sculpture, and literature. The Romans were not too proud to acknowledge this, and when they conquered the Greeks they borrowed many ideas from them. They copied Greek literature and imitated the Greek religion. A great many pieces of Greek art and sculpture were carried to Rome, and it became fashionable for the wealthy Romans to employ Greek teachers in their families. Thus while Rome conquered Greece with the sword, Greece conquered Rome with her higher intelligence.

Detail from Arch of Titus, showing Soldiers carrying the Treasures of the Temple of Jerusalem

Rome thereafter carried Grecian culture and civilization to Gaul, to England, and to Spain, and these nations transplanted the same in later centuries to America. But Rome was not only the bearer of Grecian culture; she had herself built up the finest system of law in the ancient world, and this too was carried to other nations and finally to America.

Now we come to the most important conquest of the period. Rome was conquered by Christianity, and this conquest, like that of the Greeks, was without war or bloodshed.

When Christ was born the world was at peace. Milton, in his poem on The Nativity, beautifully refers to this:

> "Nor war, or battle's sound
>   Was heard the world around;
> The idle spear and shield were high up hung.
>   The hooked chariot stood
>   Unstained with hostile blood,
> The trumpet spake not to the armed throng,
>   And Kings sat still with awful eye,
>   As if they surely knew their sov'reign Lord was by."

Rome had conquered Palestine, and at the time of the crucifixion of Christ, Pon'tius Pi'late was the Roman governor of Ju-de'a. St. Paul was born a Roman citizen in a Roman city.

When Christ's disciples went forth to preach the Gospel they had the advantage of protection by the Roman laws, which tolerated foreign religions. Paul's great missionary journeys to Asia Minor and in Greece were all within Roman territory. Often were Paul and his associates persecuted, but not by the Romans.

However, the time came when the laws of Rome worked against the Christians. When the Christians had greatly increased in numbers and had founded churches in Rome itself, there arose opposition from the government. In at least two ways, it was said, the Christians violated the Roman law — by holding secret meetings, which the law forbade, and by refusing to award divine honor to the emperor.

The Christians came to be a despised sect and often they were blamed for what they did not do. In the time of Ne′ro, when a large part of the city of Rome was burned, the Christians were blamed for setting fire to the city, and many of them were put to death. The Early Church counted ten distinct persecutions in a little over two centuries. Some of the victims were sewed up in the skins of animals and thrown to the lions in the arena of the amphitheater; others were covered from head to foot with pitch and tar and then set on fire. But the courage with which they suffered death awakened the admiration of the people and made many converts.

As time passed, the Christians became more and more numerous. It seemed that the empire was turning Christian. And just what Rome needed was a new and inspiring religion. The Roman people had lost faith in their old gods, and the morals of the nation were at a very low ebb. The brutal shows of the amphitheater in which men were slain furnished the chief delight to the gathered multitudes. The rich were degraded by the most extravagant luxury. They drove through the streets in lofty chariots followed by troops of slaves. Their horses' harness was covered with golden ornaments and precious stones. Poor people or children were often crushed by the ponderous chariot wheels; but the haughty owner cared nothing for that. The rich women wore ornaments of gold and silver so heavy that they could scarcely walk without the aid of servants. All this while thousands of the poor were homeless and starving.

THE COMING OF CHRISTIANITY 111

But the Christian religion was gradually gaining, and proud Rome, with her extravagance and wretchedness, was being conquered at last. At first the converts were among the poor, but now and then a rich woman would throw off her jewels and become a Christian.

The most noted of these was Pau'la, a woman of great wealth, a descendant of the Scipios and the Gracchi. She cast aside all her luxury; she left her fine home and went to the Holy Land. Here in the town of Bethlehem, where Christ was born, she spent twenty years living on coarse food and wearing coarse clothing, working with St. Jerome in translating the Bible into Latin. This Latin Bible, which is still used, is called the Vulgate. The translation was finished in 405 A.D.

Persecution only made the Christians stronger and more determined. At length, after the struggle had gone on for three centuries, there came an emperor named Con'stantine. He saw that the Christian religion was far superior to the worship of the old Roman gods. At length he became a convert and was baptized into the Christian Church. He also moved the capital of the empire from Rome to a city on the Bos'phor-us and called it after his own name—Con-stan'ti-no'ple.

Detail from the Arch of Constantine. Trajan sacrificing in the presence of his army

About half a century after the time of Constantine (380 A.D.) the Christian religion was made the state religion of the empire. Henceforth when Rome carried her arms and her laws and civilization to other lands, she carried the Christian religion with them. England and Germany and Gaul all became Christianized from Rome, and when these countries settled America, the settlers brought with them this same religion that had conquered Rome.

WHAT ROME GAVE TO THE WORLD

We have noticed that the Roman people, when they made their many conquests, borrowed the best things from the civilization of the peoples they conquered. Thus from Greece and Egypt they received much of their religion, until later, when they adopted Christianity from Palestine. From Greece also they adopted their systems of philosophy, much of their art, literature, and architecture. They learned much from Egypt, from Carthage, and from Etruria.

Let us notice the two most important contributions of Rome to the world to-day. First is her system of government and law. In this she excelled all other peoples of ancient times. The idea of dividing and subdividing a country so as to administer the law the better is a Roman idea. Almost all modern governments have adopted this plan. Our own country is divided into states, the states into counties, and the counties into townships, and the general idea comes from ancient Rome. In the government of the cities also, Rome set an example that has been followed by almost all modern towns.

In her system of law Rome again excelled all other peoples. It is true that her government was often corrupt and often despotic; but her laws were based on the principle of justice and fairness to all classes. The later nations of Europe all adopted the greater part of the Roman laws, and modern nations have done the same thing. Roman law is studied today in every great university in Europe and in America. No man can pretend to be a statesman, a learned judge, or lawyer who has not studied Roman law, and no state or nation makes a code of laws for its people that is not based on the laws of old Rome.

Eagle of the Roman legions

The next greatest heritage of the world from Rome is the Latin language and literature. The writings of the great Roman authors, Cæsar, Cicero, Horace, Ovid, and others, which we call classics, belong to the world's best literature. They form a part of a high school or a college education in all civilized countries.

Still more important is the enriching of the modern languages from the Latin. The French language, the Spanish, and the Italian are largely made up of Latin, while a great many English words are from the same source.

Usually the names of our dearest associations, such

as mother, father, sister, and brother, are Anglo-Saxon; while many of our more difficult terms are made up of two or more Latin words. A few examples may be interesting. Benevolent means well-wishing and is composed of two Latin words: *bene*, well, and *velere*, to wish. Manufacture is from *manus*, hand, and *facere*, to make — that is, to make by hand. The word came into use before machinery was invented, when people actually made things by hand. Aqueduct, a waterway, is from *aqua*, water, and *ducere*, to lead. Transparent comes from two Latin words: *trans*, across or through, and *parere*, to appear. Locomotive is from *locus*, a place, and *movere*, to move. Magnanimous means noble-minded, from *magnus*, great, and *animus*, mind.

Thus we see that many of our words are taken from the Latin, the language used by the Romans of olden times.

CHAPTER VI

HEIRS TO THE ROMANS

A Gaulish chief

THE Roman people, who had conquered so many nations, were never able to conquer the barbarians of northern Europe, who were called Germans. We have noticed that Caesar defeated the German leader, Ariovistus, in battle; but he did not reduce the Germans to subjection. On the other hand, the time came when the Germans conquered the Romans. Tac′i-tus, the Latin historian, described the Germans as having "stern blue eyes, ruddy hair, their bodies large and robust, but powerful only in sudden efforts."

The German tribes that invaded Italy and Spain were called Goths; those that conquered and settled in Gaul were called Franks; those that settled in Britain were known as Angles, Saxons, and Jutes. But these tribes did not remain barbarians. They found the Roman civilization better than their own and in part adopted it; and they gradually gave up their old religion. Let us notice how one of these barbarian kings became a Christian.

THE STORY OF CLOVIS

The fall of the Roman Empire dates from 476 A.D., when O-do-a′cer, a leader of a barbarian tribe, captured Rome, overthrew the emperor, and became himself king of Italy. After the year 476 there were no more Roman emperors. The empire was broken into many parts. One of these parts was Gaul, which was now occupied by the Franks, and it came to be called France.

The first great king of the Franks was Clo′vis. When he was a boy of sixteen he fell heir to a small kingdom with Tournay as its capital. There were several other small kingdoms of Franks in Gaul at this time, and Clovis determined to conquer them and unite the Franks under one strong government. It was the year 481, only six years after the fall of Rome, when Clovis became king.

Clovis
From an old print

Clovis was married to a beautiful young princess named Clotil′da, who was a daughter of the king of Burgundy. She was a Christian, but her husband was a pagan, and he had robbed many churches in his campaigns.

Clotilda begged and urged her husband to become a Christian. "The gods you worship are nothing," she said; "they cannot help themselves nor others.

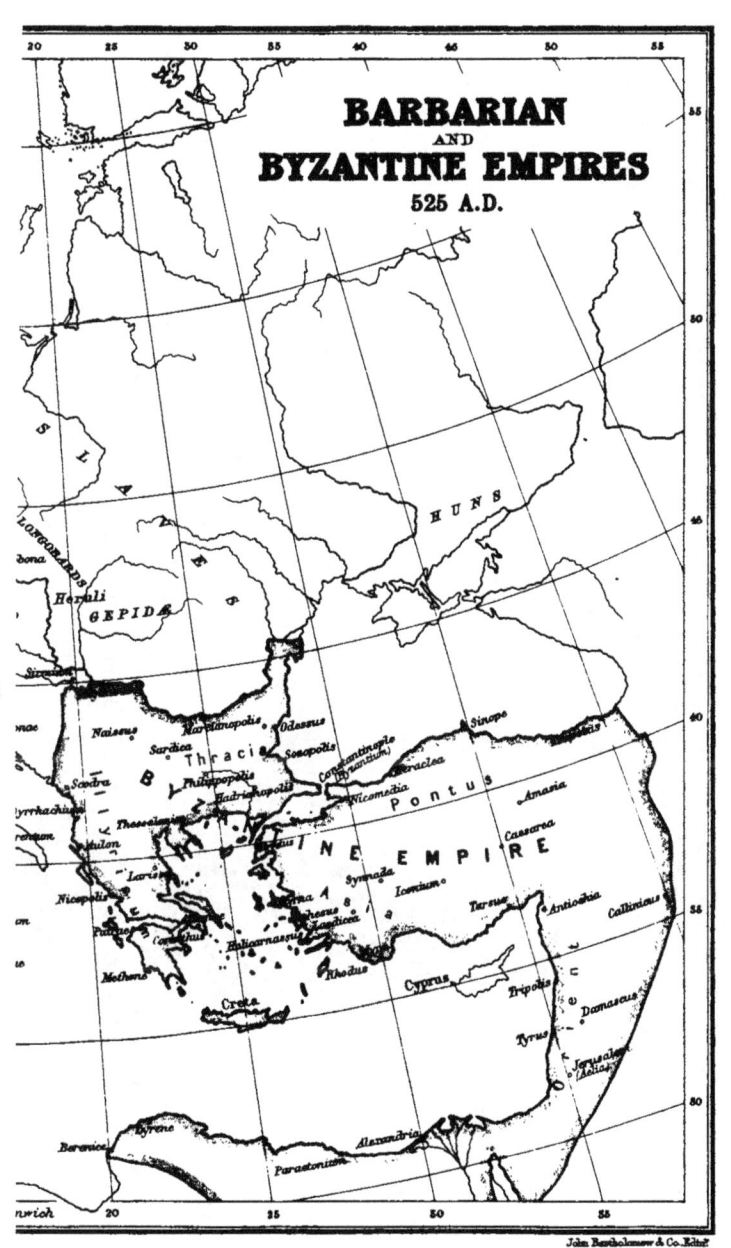

The God who should be worshiped is He who by His word created the heavens and the earth, who made the sun and adorned the sky with stars, who filled the water with creeping things, the land with animals, and the air with winged creatures."

The king was not converted, but he permitted their infant son to be baptized in the Christian faith. The child died, and Clovis believed that it was the baptism that caused its death. But when another child was born, he permitted it also to be baptized. It too became ill and the king, thinking it would die, spoke fiercely against the queen's beliefs. But Clotilda prayed fervently that the child's life be spared, and it recovered. After this Clovis was much more favorable toward the Christian religion; but he still trusted in the old gods.

Odin, a god of the early Germans

In the year 496 King Clovis was engaged in a dreadful war with the Al-e-mann'i, one of the fiercest tribes in Gaul. The battle was going against him and a great many of his brave soldiers had been slain. He had prayed to his gods in vain. As he stood on the battlefield and saw his men falling before the enemy, he burst into tears and declared that his gods were powerless to aid him. He then called on the God of Clotilda and the Christians. He prayed for success and made a vow in the midst of the fight that if he won, he would become a Christian and be baptized.

Clovis won a great victory that day, and Clotilda rejoiced exceedingly when she knew of the vow that he had made. Soon afterwards, the king, and three thousand of his men were baptized and became Christians.

In the years following, Clovis continued his conquests, and nearly all Gaul came under his dominion. He moved his capital to Paris, where he spent the remainder of his days. He was the first to unite the Franks under one rule, and to this day Clovis is looked upon as the founder of the French nation.

THE STORY OF KING ARTHUR

We Americans are more interested perhaps in the early history of England than in that of any other country on the other side of the Atlantic, as it was England that founded nearly all of our colonies.

Anglo-Saxon drinking horn in British Museum

Rome held Britain under control for about four centuries; but when the northern barbarians pressed hard on the City of the Seven Hills, the Roman armies had to be withdrawn from Britain. During those four centuries the British people had lost the art of war, and they were not able to defend themselves against the barbarian hordes that landed on their shores. The Jutes came in 449, led by two brothers, Hen′gist and Hor′sa. The Saxons arrived about thirty years later, and the Angles still later. When the Angles came, they brought with them their women and children, intending to remain. It was this tribe that gave its name to the island — Angle-Land, or England. Before this, the island was known as Britain and its people as Britons.

The war between these German tribes and the Britons was long and fierce. It lasted nearly one hundred and fifty years and ended with a complete victory for the Germans. Let us notice one incident of this long war — the battle of Badon Hill and its hero, King Arthur. It is probable that the story of Arthur is founded in fact. But a wonderful web of legend has been woven around his name.

According to these legends Arthur had twelve brave knights who sat with him at a round table, and they were called "The Knights of the Round Table." They went forth into various countries seeking adventure, and their heroic deeds furnish the subjects of many stories of the Middle Ages.

The battle of Badon Hill, probably about the year 500, was one of the greatest ever fought between the Britons and the Saxons. Arthur was king of the Britons. On his spirited war-steed he rode among his troops and cheered them on to battle. The legend tells us that he slew nine hundred and forty of the enemy with his own hand. The Britons won the day. Many thousands of the Saxons were slain, and it was forty years before they fully recovered from their fearful defeat at Badon Hill.

Arthur was the hero of many battles. In the last of these he was covered with wounds and was borne away from the field by fairy hands to a beautiful

England and the continent whence came her many invaders

enchanted island called Avalon. Here he died and was buried, but the legend said he would rise again and return to deliver the people from their enemies.

Tennyson's "Idyls of the King" is based on the legends of Arthur. In these lines the poet refers to the burial place of the hero, —

> "To the island-valley of Avilion,
> Where falls not hail, or rain or any snow,
> Nor ever wind blows loudly; but it lies
> Deep-meadowed, happy, fair with orchard lawns,
> And bowery hollows crowned with summer sea."

Within a century after the German tribes had conquered the Britons and had taken possession of the land, they became converted to Christianity. Augustine, sent by Pope Gregory, landed in England in 597 and began to preach the Gospel of Christ. In less than half a century nearly the whole country was converted and churches rose on all sides.

"The present life of man on earth," said an officer of the army, "seems to me like the swift flight of a sparrow through the room where you sit at supper in winter. While the storms prevail outside, the sparrow flies in at one door and out at another; whilst it is within it is safe from the wintry storm, but it soon vanishes into the dark whence it came. So this life of man appears for a short space, but of what went before and what is to follow we are ignorant. If therefore this new religion contains something more certain it seems to deserve to be followed." And one old pagan priest cried out, "I have long believed that there was nothing in that which we worshiped, because the more I sought after truth, the less I found it." And this aged priest was the first to destroy the altars and temples of the heathen gods.

THE VIKINGS

After the conversion of England there was prosperity for a long season. But the country was divided into several small kingdoms. Part of the time there were seven of these, and after various wars with one another they were united into one, under King Egbert, about the year 827. This one was called the Hep′tarchy, which means seven kingdoms.

At this time, and even earlier, the English people had to contend with a dangerous foe — the Danes. Three hundred years had passed since the island had been invaded by foreigners, and the people were not prepared to defend their country. The Danes and Northmen from Scandinavia therefore found them an easy prey.

These hardy seamen of the north, often called Vikings, almost lived on the water. In their high-prowed boats, they traversed all the northern seas, defying the rolling billows and the storm. Moreover, they were reckless robbers; they had little idea of the rights of life and property, and woe to the hapless inhabitants of the coasts they ravaged. It was the descendants of these same Northmen who, two hundred years later, settled Greenland and, led by Leif Ericson, became the first Europeans to discover North America.

A Danish War-ship

At first these daring rovers of the sea ravaged only the coasts of Britain. They would swoop down on the coast towns during the summer months, rob and pillage the inhabitants, and then sail swiftly back to their northern home before winter. But at length they ascended the rivers and made settlements. The

English fought them, but were unable to drive them out. Sometimes they made terms with the Danes and purchased peace by paying them money. But the latter often forgot their agreements and again crowded the English from their homes. And when Alfred, the grandson of Egbert, became king, the Danes occupied a large portion of northern and eastern England, and the line between them and the English they called the Danelagh.

ALFRED BECOMES KING

Alfred, like David, king of Israel, was the youngest and the fairest of the sons of his father. Alfred's father was Eth'-elwulf, king of Wessex and Kent; a large part of the remainder of England was under the control of the Danes. The prince was born in 849, and being the youngest, it was thought that he would never come to the throne. His education was there-

Alfred the Great

fore neglected, though he was very eager to learn. The story tells us that when Alfred was about twelve years old his mother showed him and his brothers a book of Anglo-Saxon poetry and said, "Whichever of you will learn this book first shall have it for his own." Alfred was delighted at this opportunity to own a book. He studied diligently and he won the reward over his older brothers. There were no printing-presses in those days, and a book printed by hand was a rare and costly prize.

King Ethelwulf took his young son Alfred with him on a pilgrimage to Rome. They stopped for some time at Paris, the guests of the king. We can imagine what a life-long impression was made on the mind of the young English prince by the brilliant court of the French king and the wonderful city on the Tiber.

We are told that as a boy Alfred became very skilful in hunting, riding, and in the use of the bow and arrow; but that, as he found his body becoming so perfect, he prayed that God would give him some illness. Soon after this he was afflicted with a painful disease. Whether this story is true or not we do not know. But it is true that Alfred, all through the years of his manhood, suffered from a disease which the doctors of that day did not understand. In spite of this, however, he showed wonderful vigor and energy.

Early hand-printed book chained to a desk

Alfred had three brothers older than himself, all of whom wore the crown. The eldest died after a reign of two years and the second after he had reigned six years. The third was Eth'elred, who then succeeded to the crown, and the records seem to show that Alfred was associated with him in governing the country.

About this time the invasion by the Danes was at its height. A large army of them landed on the coast of Kent, near the mouth of the Thames River. It was the year 871. They pushed on into the interior and met the English, led by the royal brothers, near Reading. After they had fought for a time, the English thought that they had won a victory and were preparing to encamp for the night, when the Danes suddenly rushed upon them and put them to flight. But this did not end the contest.

A few days after the affair at Reading the two armies met at Ashdown, a place in Berkshire, and here was fought the decisive battle of the war. The men of both sides believed that on this day would be decided the fate of England. Here on the chalk hills, one cold night in March, the opposing armies built their watch fires in view of each other. On the morrow the clash of arms would come.

Next morning at break of day the hosts of both sides were astir. King Ethelred had divided the English army into two parts, retaining one himself and giving the other to Alfred. The Danes made an immediate attack on Alfred's division. This was the supreme moment of the young prince's life. If on this day he should fail or falter, England would be lost and the barbarians would overrun the whole land. But Alfred did not falter.

"With the rush of a wild boar," said an eye-witness, "he dashed up the slope at the head of his men, arranging them in a phalanx." There was an old thorn tree around which the battle raged. For many hours the clash of arms resounded from hill to hill. Alfred seemed to be everywhere, cheering his men and striking down the enemy with his own hand.

All day long the slaughter continued, and toward evening a shout was heard from the English lines. The Danes were giving way. At length they broke and fled; but they left thousands of their men dead and dying scattered along the hillsides. Two Danish kings had led the pagans; one of them was lying dead among his men.

Some say that King Ethelred received a fatal wound in this battle; others, that it was in another a little later. It is certain that he died soon after the battle of Ashdown. Who should succeed to the throne of England? Ethelred left sons; but they were children. The times needed a man, a strong, fearless, able man — and here he was — Alfred.

An English Crossbow Man
From an old print

THE GREATEST OF THE ENGLISH KINGS

In the history of England there has been but one king to whose name "The Great" has been attached. It was Alfred, who reigned thirty years, from 871 to

901. He laid the foundations of the British educational system, the British navy, and the British Empire. No man that ever lived deserved more than he to be called "The Great."

The Danes were defeated at Ashdown by the great skill and prowess of Alfred, but they were not driven from the country. The English king was slain, and Alfred became monarch at the age of twenty-three. The people adored their young king and clung around him as their only hope of deliverance from the barbarian hordes of the north.

Collecting and training his men as best he could, Alfred met the invaders on many a bloody field. Nine times in one year the armies met and fought, and the English were usually successful owing to the skill of their royal commander. But the Danes came in ever increasing numbers. Bands of them overran the fair lands and left a trail of desolation. One writer of the time said, "The land was as the Garden of Eden before them, and behind them a desolate wilderness."

There were moments when the great soul of Alfred was cast down with discouragement. At one time, with a few followers, he took refuge in the fens and bogs of Somersetshire and suffered for want of food. The story is told that he found a refuge in the cabin of a herdsman, where he remained several days, the family not knowing who he was. One day when the housewife was baking cakes, she asked her guest to watch them a few minutes during her absence. The king was so busy making bows and arrows that he did not notice when the cakes began to burn. When the woman returned she upbraided him saying, "Why not turn the cakes when you see they are burning? You are glad enough to eat them when they are baked."

It is also related that Alfred disguised himself as a wandering minstrel and went into the Danish camp to find out the numbers and intentions of the enemy. But there is no proof that this story is true.

The Danish king who contended so long with Alfred was named Guth'rum. At length he promised that the southern part of England, Alfred's kingdom, should be free from the invaders. And for a number of years he kept his word.

No ruler ever labored more faithfully than Alfred to raise the standard of education and religion among his people. He complained that not a person south of the Thames River could read Latin, and after he was forty years old Alfred learned that language himself so that he could translate Latin literature into Anglo-Saxon. Two of the translations that he made were Bede's History of the Church and a Guide for pastors of the churches.

King Alfred was himself very religious. He would attend church service every day and humbly kneel in prayer with his subjects. He would often rise in the night and go alone to the church and spend several hours in secret prayer.

Alfred gave his people a code of wise laws. He was a student of science and did all he could to encourage others to investigate things unknown. He devised new plans for building houses; he discovered a way to tell time by the use of lighted candles of a uniform size; he taught craftsmen about their own craft and how to excel in it. He sent to Gaul for learned men to come to his kingdom and become the teachers of himself and his people.

King Alfred and his Candle-clock

In all that we can learn about King Alfred, there is no record that he ever did a cruel or mean act. He loved his people as his own family. A great historian has used these words in describing this prince among rulers: "No other man on record has ever so thoroughly united all the virtues both of ruler and of the private man. A saint without superstition, a scholar without boast, a warrior whose wars were fought in defense of his own country, a conqueror whose laurels were never stained by cruelty, a prince never cast down by adversity, never lifted up to insolence in the hour of triumph — there is no other name in history to compare with his."

BEGINNINGS OF AMERICAN LIBERTY

The English people were hundreds of years establishing liberty and self-government. They succeeded in the end, and their victory was our victory also, for in later times, when English people settled in America, they brought with them the spirit of liberty and a knowledge of self-government. How did they win these rights? Let us see.

It must be remembered that all rulers are not Alfreds. If they were, nobody would ever need to strive or fight for liberty. England had kings in later years who were selfish and tyrannical, caring nothing for the welfare of the people. Against them the people had to rise and assert their rights.

The Danes did not cease coming to the island with the time of Alfred. They continued to come and to make war on the English. But the time came when the wars ceased. The Danes were converted to Christianity, they made friends with the English, and the two peoples then lived in harmony, and all of them came to be known as one people.

A little more than two hundred years after the birth of King Alfred, there took place the most memorable single event in the history of England. It is known as the Norman Conquest and its date is 1066.

The Normans were the people of Normandy, a portion of northern France. They had come from the north as had the Danes. The word Normans means Northmen, and Normandy means the home of the Northmen.

The duke of Normandy was a powerful ruler named William. He claimed the English throne on the death of the aged king in 1066, though the English people had chosen Harold as their king. William crossed the channel with a great fleet bearing an army of sixty thousand men.

King Harold hastened to gather an army and meet the invaders. The two great armies met on the Senlac Hills not far from Hastings, a town in Sussex near the channel coast. Then occurred, on October 14th, 1066, the most famous of all English battles

A Norman Invader

— the battle of Hastings. All day long the two great armies contended in bloody strife. A writer of the time says, "You could hear the sound of many trumpets, loud and far-resounding the bray of bugles and horns; and the shocks of the lances, the mighty strokes of the maces, and the quick clashings of swords."

Which side would win was uncertain, until evening. About sundown King Harold received an arrow in the eye, which pierced his brain. He was soon dead, and his disheartened army was defeated and scattered. William had won the crown of England. He is known as William the Conqueror. He reigned over England to the end of his life, and his sons and grandsons after him.

William the Conqueror
From an ancient effigy

The Norman kings took away from the English people the liberties they had enjoyed under such kings as Alfred. They were now ground down with tyranny and with heavy taxation. At length there came a king who to this day is pronounced the most wicked ruler that England ever had. His name was John. He first tried to steal his brother Richard's kingdom, while the latter was absent on a crusade to the Holy Land. In his absence Richard had entrusted his kingdom to John, but John proved a traitor to the trust and tried to defraud his elder brother of his rights. He was humble enough, however, when his brother returned. A few years later Richard died, in 1199, and John became the real king of England.

But it was not long before he quarreled with the Church, with the barons or nobles, and with his people.

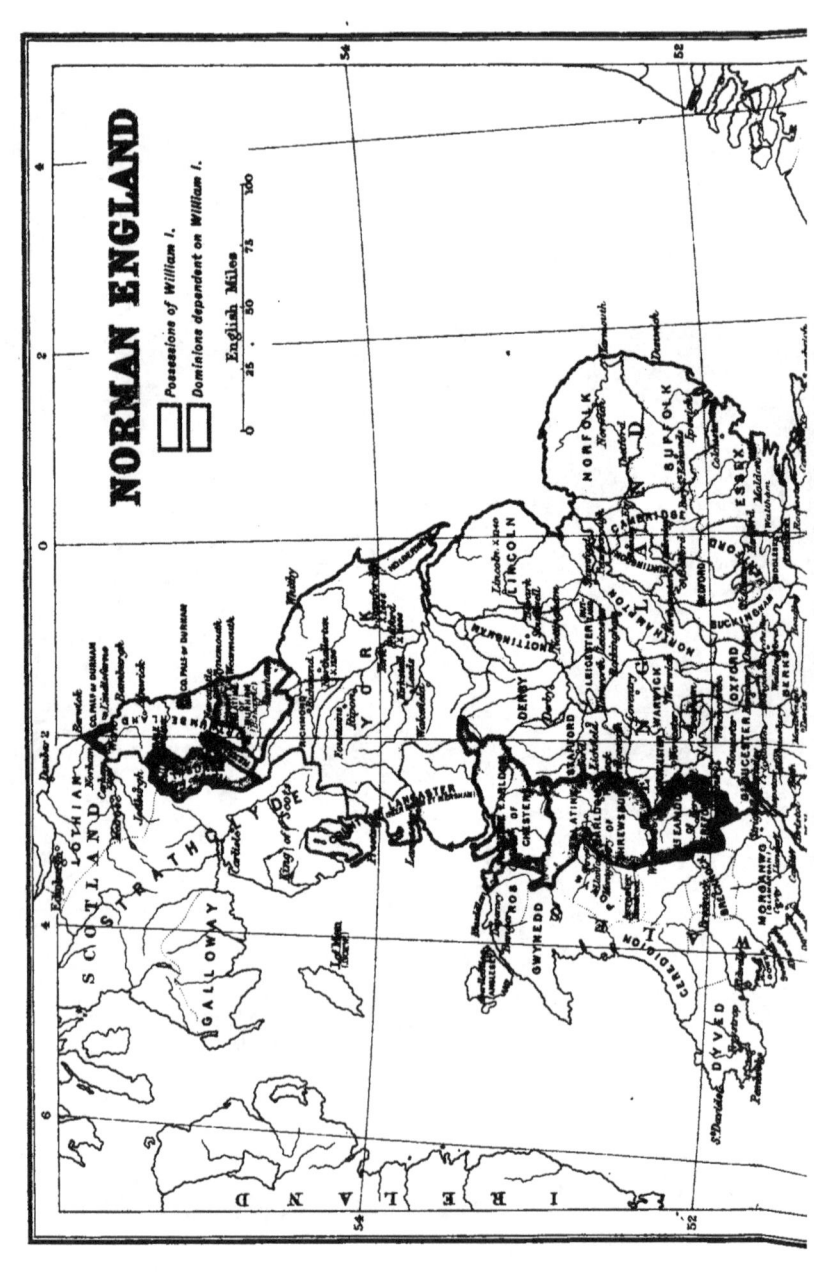

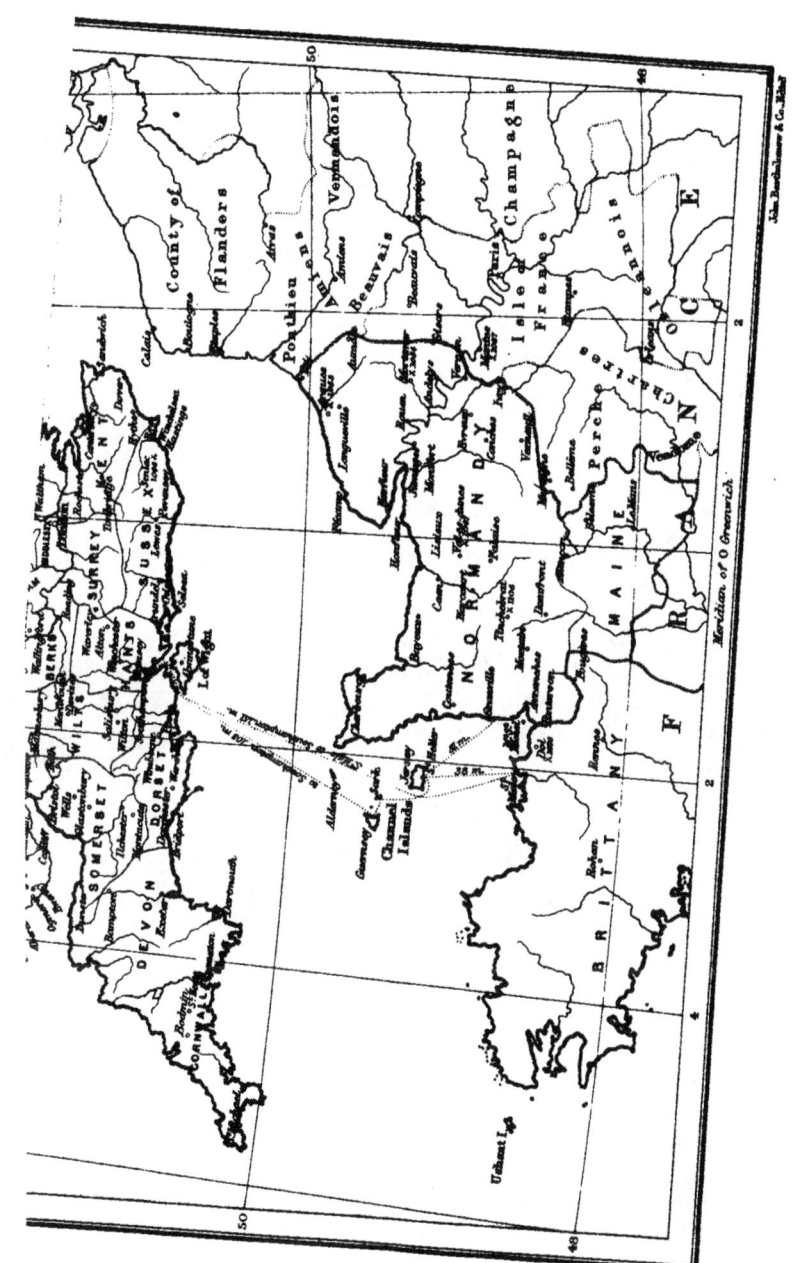

He was heartless and cruel. To keep the barons from going against him he would take their children, keep them in his palace, and threaten to kill them if their fathers did not do as he wished, and in several cases he carried out his threat. He murdered his brother's little son, Prince Arthur, in prison; at least, everyone believed that he did it, and it is still so believed. He would cast men into prison on some false charge and then make them pay a large sum of money to secure a trial.

The people at length decided that they would not suffer such cruel actions any longer. Led by a great man, Stephen Langton, Archbishop of Can'ter-bu-ry, the barons rose in rebellion. At St. Edmundsbury they held a meeting and took a solemn oath that if the king did not yield to their claims of just government, they would withdraw their allegiance. They then armed themselves and marched upon London to make their

William the Conqueror embarking
From the Bayeux tapestry

demands. John flew into a rage and refused their requests. He fled from London, and was driven from place to place. The barons had drawn up a charter, or an agreement, which they were determined he should sign. At length they overtook the fleeing monarch at a place called Run'ny-mede on the Thames, and here he signed the articles.

The agreement has since been known as the Magna Charta (the Latin for Great Charter). It was signed by King John on June 15th, 1215, a great date in English history. It provided that the people should not be taxed without their consent, that no one should be imprisoned or banished except by the law of the land, and that justice should not be sold or denied to anyone.

King John

The king had been forced to sign the great charter, and afterwards he was so angry at what he had done that he rolled on the floor and gnawed sticks and straws in his fury. He soon decided, however, that he would not keep his promise, and, collecting an army, he marched against the barons. They thereupon appealed to France for help, and a son of the French king crossed the channel with an army.

There was now civil war, but suddenly, the next year, 1216, it came to an end when King John died.

The Magna Charta is the greatest document of its kind in the world. It is to this day the basis of English liberty, and of ours also, because we Americans inherited our liberty from England.

THE ENGLISH PARLIAMENT

When King John died his son Henry inherited the throne of England. He is known in history as Henry III. He was only nine years of age at the time of his father's death, and a regent was appointed to govern until the young king was old enough to rule.

The people believed that Henry would be a better ruler than his father, and the time came when they had an opportunity to see. The barons or noblemen who had forced King John to sign the Great Charter were powerful in England, and Henry knew it. He would call them together whenever he needed money, and he would give them special privileges if they would grant his request for funds. This assembly of the barons was called a Parliament (from the French word meaning "speaking").

John's Anger after signing the Magna Charta

But the noblemen soon learned their lesson. The queen of England was a French woman, and King Henry was foolishly spending money on his French friends. The people rebelled against the heavy taxes, and there soon came a time when Parliament refused his request for funds. Among the barons was the Earl Simon de Mont'fort, Henry's brother-in-law. Although the earl was a Frenchman by birth, he was determined to have a better government for the English. De Montfort led a party against the king, and Henry had reason to tremble. "Am I your prisoner?" he asked. "No, you are our king," was the answer. "We will obey you if you treat us fairly."

De Montfort then called a Parliament in the king's name; and to this assembly were asked, not only the bishops and nobles, but other citizens and the country gentlemen. This was in 1265, and it marks the beginning of the lower house of the law-making body in England to-day — the House of Commons. It was decided that there should be regular meetings of Parliament to discuss the affairs of the government.

It was not long, however, before wars occurred between De Montfort's party and the king's, and in the battle of Eves'ham the earl was slain. But an old ballad tells us that

> "— by his death Earl Simon hath
> In sooth the victory won."

And the words of the ballad are true, for it was largely through the efforts of Simon de Montfort that the people came to have representation in Parliament.

King Henry had a weak character and he was as untruthful as his father had been, but he was not so

THE ENGLISH PARLIAMENT

mean and selfish. He ruled for more than fifty years and at his death his son Edward succeeded to the throne. This king is known in history as Edward I. He wished to regain a province that the king of France had taken. But as he had no money to raise an army, he tried to force men into the service. "You shall either go or be hanged," he said to a certain nobleman. "I will neither go nor yet will I be hanged," was the reply. Then what did Edward do? He began to tax the people. He told them that he would allow their property to be seized unless they would give him money.

But the barons and bishops would not permit such conduct. They declared that they would not help him nor would they give him money unless he would promise

Robert Bruce
From the picture at Taymouth, by Jamieson

that no taxes should be collected without the consent of Parliament. He agreed to this and he adopted the Earl of Montfort's idea by admitting to his Parliament not only the nobles and bishops but representatives from the towns. About fifty years later Parliament was divided into two houses, the upper house and the lower house — the House of Lords and the House of Commons.

THE WELSH AND THE SCOTS

Edward was a much stronger king than his father, and although he liked to do as he pleased he was a just ruler. He ordered that all coins should be made round. Before this English pennies were cut into halves and quarters for half-pence and farthings. Now the people of Wales were happy, for there was a prophecy handed down from Mer'lin, the magician of King Arthur's court, that a Welsh prince would be crowned in England when all the coins were round.

The Welsh were proud that they were Britons, and they hoped that some day such a king as Arthur would rule them. They rebelled against the English, but they yielded when Edward told them that he would give them a prince born in their own country to govern them. We can imagine their delight when he added that this prince could speak not a word of English. But their joy did not last long, for the prince was Edward's infant son, who had been born in Wales a few weeks before. Since then the eldest son of the English ruler has received the title of "Prince of Wales."

Edward tried to conquer the Scotch, but in this he was not successful. He carried back, however, to England the Stone of Scone upon which the kings of Scotland were crowned. There is an old ballad that tells us

> "Unless the fates are faithless found
> And prophet's voice be vain,
> Where'er is placed this stone, e'en there
> The Scottish race shall reign."

This stone is still preserved. It forms the support of the chair on which the English ruler sits at his coronation.

Robert Bruce was crowned king of Scotland, but Edward defeated him and drove him into Ireland. Bruce had reasons to be discouraged: six times he had tried to save Scotland and six times he had failed. "I will not try again," he said to himself. He had no sooner said this than he noticed a spider trying to weave a web. Six times the little creature had lost its hold as it was trying to fasten its thread. "If it tries once more and is successful, I will make another effort," said Bruce. The spider was successful and Robert Bruce had learned his lesson, and the English were defeated in the battle of Bannockburn.

About four hundred years later, in 1707, Scotland united with England, and since then both countries have representatives in one Parliament.

THE MANOR OF THE MIDDLE AGES

At the close of a period known in Old World history as the Middle Ages the common people were gradually asserting themselves, and the result of this in England was the introduction of the House of Commons, so called because it represented the common people. Let us look into the life of the people of this period.

A Medieval Fortress

In the eleventh century, at the time of the Norman Conquest, it was thought that the king owned all the land in England, and the lords and barons were his vassals or servants. The king would grant an estate to a noble on the condition that the baron would render his royal master some service in return. The estate was called a manor (from the Latin word meaning "to dwell"). Our word "mansion" comes from the same Latin term.

As war was the chief business of the barons, the most valuable service that a lord could render his master was to contribute soldiers for the king's army. But where would the nobleman get the warriors? The lord in turn granted portions of his estate to gentlemen of lower rank, called knights, and as military service was required of every man of rank, these knights were bound to furnish armed and mounted soldiers to fight the battles of the king.

On taking the oath of loyalty the vassal would place his hands in those of his master and kneel down before him, promising to defend his lord against an enemy and to be faithful to his vow. The master would then raise him and acknowledge him as his vassal by giving him a kiss. But if the servant proved unfaithful to his pledge his land was taken away and given to another.

Head-dress in the Eleventh Century

Who plowed the fields and tilled the soil of the manor? This was done by the serfs. They were different from slaves, as their service was attached to the land on which they lived and was transferred with it. They were sometimes called villeins (from the Latin word meaning a village. Our word "villain" comes from the same Latin term).

Each serf had a little plot of ground which his overlord had given him for service rendered; and he not only tilled his own soil, but for three days in the week he worked on his lord's land. But he was asked to do more than this; he was required to bring to the manor house some of the produce of his own little plot, and he was often compelled to take care of his lord's cattle and sheep. It is true he was allowed to grind his corn in his lord's mill and bake his bread in his lord's oven, but he was forced to pay for these privileges in labor. Then, too, there was an overseer to direct the serf's labor upon his lord's estate, and to see that he brought the produce in on the stated day.

Such a relation which existed between vassal and lord was called the feudal system. The word "feud" comes from an old French term meaning "property"; but as strife arose between master and servant the word to-day means "a quarrel."

The serfs of the Middle Ages were of all classes the most wretched. A time came, however, when they rebelled, and their condition was improved, for the lords realized that it was to the master's interest to protect those who supported him. Later there were contracts entered into by both parties, and in this way the

Three Peasants of the Sixteenth Century
Drawn by Dürer

serfs came to pay a stated rent for their property; and still later there came a day when there were landlords and tenants with leases for short terms or long terms.

THE WALLED TOWN

There were times when a serf would run away from the manor and find employment within the walls of a town. Some of these walls date back to the Roman days. An inscribed tablet on an old wall in London to-day calls attention to the fact that it was built by the Romans centuries ago. There are other fragments in the city of the same wall which once surrounded the town. And some of the streets in London mark the localities of the old gates which led into the walled city, such as Newgate, Cripplegate, and Ludgate.

A Tournament in the Middle Ages
From an old print

Outside the bounds of the city walls William the Conqueror erected a tower to overawe the citizens of London. It stands on the bank of the Thames (temz) and was first a royal palace and stronghold. Later other buildings were added to it, and it became a prison which we know in history as the Tower of London. It is now used as a government arsenal.

The lord's castle also had a strong tower where he and his family dwelt in time of danger. On the main floor of the castle was the dining hall where the noble entertained his guests. Underneath the hall was the gloomy dungeon where offenders were imprisoned. Around the tower was a fortress wall and outside of this a ditch or moat. Over it was a drawbridge and there was a portcullis made of strong iron bars that could suddenly be dropped in case of surprise.

The inhabitants of the city would combine to defend their walls. But this was not the only union; the merchants and artisans would form associations to protect their manufactures and trades. These were called gilds, and at one time there were as many as a hundred such unions in London. There were the Fishmongers, the Haberdashers, the Drapers, the Goldsmiths, and the Grocers. Some of the gilds would give plays at different corners of the streets presenting stories from the Bible, and their stage was a three-story wagon representing hell, earth, and heaven.

Many of the gilds would meet in halls in which they transacted business and held festivities; and among the most interesting buildings to-day in London are the old gild-halls, where the associations are still kept up, but they no longer exercise their ancient privileges.

TRAINING FOR KNIGHTHOOD

Closely associated with the feudal times is chivalry or the system of knighthood. All men might aspire to the honors of knighthood, but usually the title was given only to nobles. The young nobleman was left in the care of his mother until he was seven years of age. The boy played marbles and battledore and he learned to ride a horse, for the best horseman is he who has ridden from childhood, and a knight was required to ride well.

After seven years of age the youth was sent to the castle of some great nobleman, and here he served as a page. And now what were his duties? He waited upon the ladies of the castle, and he entertained them by singing songs and playing upon the lute. He learned to be courteous, brave, and truthful. He was trained to be strong and his exercises were fencing and hunting.

At fourteen years of age he became a squire, and then until he was twenty he attended the knights in tournaments. These were exhibitions in which there were tilts with lances. Two opposing parties of knights would contend on horseback with blunted weapons, and the art of the contest consisted in the rider's turning his horse so as to avoid the opponent's blow. A lady of high rank

A Tilt with Lances

would generally award the prize to the victor. The squire helped the knight to put on his armor or to raise him when he had fallen from his horse. These tournaments were fought vigorously. Accidents often happened. In one such tourney a king of France, Henry II, was killed.

When the candidate's apprenticeship was ended, he was ready to enter into the order of chivalry. The title of knighthood might be conferred on the field of battle, but it was more often given during one of the great Church festivals, such as Christmas, Easter, or Whitsuntide. No one could take the title who was not a Christian or who was not willing to fight for his church and country.

Before the candidate received the title he went to the church and there he spent a day and a night in prayer and fasting. His armor was laid upon the altar and the priest blessed it. Now the candidate was prepared to make his vow to be a valiant knight. As he knelt before the altar he swore that he would right all wrong, that he would honor all women, and that he would protect the weak and defenseless. Then a knight of high rank drew his sword and struck the candidate saying, "I dub thee knight in the name of God and in the name of the King." This light blow and salutation was called the accolade.

The ceremony was now ended and the newly made knight arose and received the formal kiss into the order of chivalry. Ladies of high degree helped him to put on his spurs and armor, and he then sprang upon his horse and rode from the church.

THE CANTERBURY CATHEDRAL

During the Middle Ages labor and money were not spared to build beautiful churches and cathedrals. Years and years passed before they were completed. In the old Greek temples the columns played an important part in architecture, but in the Middle Ages there was the pointed style with its crosses and spires. These cathedrals still stand as places for worship, and many thousands and thousands of people from different countries visit them every year.

The Canterbury Cathedral in England dates back to the Middle Ages. In 1170 Thomas à Becket was Archbishop of Canterbury. He was at first friendly with the king, Henry II, but they did not remain long on good terms, and the archbishop opposed the king. In a moment of anger Henry cried, "What a pack of cowards I have in my court. Not one will rid me of this upstart priest."

Canterbury Cathedral

He had no sooner said this than four knights hastened to Canterbury and there in the cathedral they sought their victim. "Where is Thomas à Becket, the traitor?" they cried. "Here I am," exclaimed the archbishop as he came forward. "I am no traitor to the king," he said, "I am a priest." Heavy blows followed and soon the Archbishop of Canterbury lay dead at the altar. "He will rise up no more," cried the knights as they fled from the cathedral.

But in this they were mistaken, for Thomas à Becket dead was even more powerful than alive. The Church cried out in horror at the murder of the archbishop and he became the most popular of saints. His body was placed in a large and stately tomb in the cathedral, and many thousands of pilgrims have knelt at the martyr's shrine.

Before the Middle Ages closed Geoffrey Chaucer, the father of English poetry, wrote the "Canterbury Tales." They are stories that the pilgrims tell on their journey to the shrine of Thomas à Becket, and the one who tells the best story is to have a supper at the expense of the others. But the worn stone steps of the Canterbury Cathedral to-day also tell a story.

Nor must we forget the monasteries of the Middle Ages. Many of the monks were workers in the improvement of land and they taught the people how to till their fields to better advantage. They gave instruction in glass-making and wood-carving. Students went to the monasteries to study Latin, and there to read the Latin authors. Books were not printed in those days, but written on parchment scrolls by the monks, who also translated the old manuscripts. All this required years of labor, and it is largely due to the work of the monasteries that ancient literature has come down to us.

CHAPTER VII

THE CRUSADES

IN the Middle Ages the Christians of Europe made pilgrimages to Jerusalem, the Holy City where Christ had lived. The Arabs had conquered the Holy Land. They were not Christians but Mo-ham'med-ans. Their Bible was the Koran, the recorded teachings of their religious leader, Mohammed.

Many of the Arabs worshiped idols, but Mohammed believed that there was one Supreme Being — Allah. He recognized Christ as a prophet of God, but he proclaimed himself as a greater prophet. He would often wander to the desert, and there in a cave he would pray and meditate. He told of a vision that had come to him while he was thus praying. An angel appeared with a silken banner and on it the words were written in gold. "Read," said the heavenly messenger. Mohammed had never learned to read, but as he was looking at the writing, there suddenly came to him the power to interpret the words. They revealed to him, he said, a higher religion than had ever been preached, and he was commanded by the angel to teach it to his people.

He began to preach in Mecca, his native city, but here he had many enemies, and he and his disciples fled to Me-di'na, another city in Arabia. Even to this day the Mohammedans do not reckon their time from the birth of Christ as we do, but from Mohammed's flight to Medina, which took place six hundred and twenty-two years after the birth of Christ.

At Medina, Mohammed ordered a temple to be built, called a mosque. Here he preached and assembled the people five times a day for prayer. And although it is more than a thousand years since he lived, his followers in the East still obey the call, "Come to prayers! God is great and Mohammed is his prophet." And as they pray they turn their faces toward Mecca, the birthplace of their prophet.

Mohammed
From an old print
(Traditional likeness)

The Arabs, however, were kind to the Christians when they came to Jerusalem, and gave them protection when they made their pilgrimages to the sepulcher of their Lord. But there came a time when the Turks, who were also Mohammedans, conquered the Arabs and obtained possession of Jerusalem. They were fierce and cruel, and they either put the Christian pilgrims to death or made them endure terrible torture.

THE FIRST CRUSADE

In the latter part of the eleventh century, Pope Urban at Rome made an appeal to the Christians of Europe to deliver Jerusalem, their Holy City, from the Turks. The Pope had been moved to action by the preaching of Peter the Hermit. He went to Clermont in France, and there in an open field he spoke to a large gathering of people — lords and knights, squires and pages, merchants and peasants. Indeed, men in every station of life came to listen to him.

Peter the Hermit preaching the First Crusade
From a painting by Archer

He told them that the Holy City was now in the hands of unbelievers and that Christians were murdered within the Church of the Holy Sepulcher and that the City must be saved. He had hardly concluded when that vast assembly cried out, "God wills it! God wills it!" "Let that be your battle cry," said the pope. And then he gave each a blood-red cross. "Wear it upon your shoulder as a symbol of your zeal in the service of Christ," he said.

It was not many months after Pope Urban's appeal that a vast number of Christians set out to deliver Jerusalem from the cruel Turks. Such a movement was called a crusade (from the Latin word *crux*, meaning a cross). These crusaders took neither money nor food with them. The pope had told them that God would take care of them, and he chose as their leader the French monk who had first suggested the crusades.

This monk was called Peter the Hermit because he had deserted the world and lived in seclusion. He was a small man with a long white beard and deep, searching eyes. Late in life he made a pilgrimage to Jerusalem, and one morning while he was praying before the Holy Sepulcher, he thought he heard a voice saying, "Peter, arise! Hasten to tell France of the suffering of God's people!" When he returned to his native country he proclaimed the cruelty of the Turks and told of the Christian martyrs. He would journey from place to place, mounted upon a mule and wearing a coarse woolen mantle. And Pope Urban said, "Peter the Hermit is the man to lead the crusade."

In the spring the impatient crowd of more than sixty thousand set out on their journey to Jerusalem. Peter the Hermit had no easy task in leading these people. Some went for selfish reasons — to see new countries and to plunder. There were robbers and thieves among this marching crowd. A goose and a goat were led at the head of the procession, for it was thought that these creatures had wisdom beyond the knowledge of man. There was order for a time, and all went well. The pilgrims passed through Germany, and the people gave them food. But as they journeyed on into Hungary and Bulgaria, they were attacked by the rude inhabitants, and the crusaders took revenge upon the people who refused to supply them with provisions. There were bloody fights, and more than thirty thousand that had set out for Jerusalem perished.

At length the remaining pilgrims reached Constantinople, where the Greek Emperor Alexius allowed them to pitch their camp to wait for new bands of crusaders. They did not seem to appreciate the emperor's kindness, for they plundered not only houses but churches. He was, indeed, glad to get rid of them, and he induced them to go on. Before they started out again they were reenforced by great numbers of Germans and Italians.

They now marched on, and in time came to the territory of the Turks. "God wills it! God wills it!" was the cry. It was not long before a terrible battle took place on the plains of Nice. But the Turks were victorious and slaughtered the Christians unmercifully.

Of these first crusaders more than two hundred thousand perished, and yet Jerusalem was not delivered from the infidels.

But the crusades did not cease. There now arose another leader, Godfrey of Bouillon, a French nobleman of great strength. There was not the disorderly crowd this time, but there were four large armies well organized. They passed through Germany, crossed the plains of Hungary, and fought their way through mountain passes. Finally they reached Constantinople, and there they were joined by Peter the Hermit, for he had escaped to that city.

Tomb of Godfrey de Bouillon

Later they all marched on toward Jerusalem. Many were killed on the way in battle, and many died of hunger and thirst. But they were sincere in their purpose, and they chanted as they marched, "Let the Lord arise, and let his enemies be scattered." At length they came within sight of the Holy City, and it was not long before a siege was begun. For forty days it lasted, and proved successful. Godfrey erected the cross, the standard of the Christian soldiers, on the walls of Jerusalem.

At last the Holy City was delivered from the Turks, but not without a terrible massacre, and in that dark age the Christian knights were as brutal as the infidels. Their one thought was to save Jerusalem. "God wills it! God wills it!" they cried. And as they entered the city they were wild with joy. They took off their shoes, and fell upon their knees, kissing the ground where Christ once trod.

And now who was to rule the Holy City? Ten electors were appointed to choose a king, and Godfrey was their choice. But he refused the royal title, saying, "I will not wear a crown of gold in the city where Christ wore a crown of thorns." He was willing, however, to accept the title of Defender of the Holy Sepulcher, and he solemnly pledged himself to rule with justice and honor.

After a time most of the crusaders returned to their homes. The others remained with Godfrey in Jerusalem. No one rejoiced more that the Holy City was saved than Peter the Hermit. He returned to France and spent his last years in a monastery.

KING RICHARD AND THE THIRD CRUSADE

The Christians had control of Jerusalem for more than eighty years when it fell again into the hands of the Mohammedans. There was a second crusade, led by the king of France and the emperor of Germany, but it ended in failure.

The Christians of Europe, however, did not give up. Later there was a third expedition to the Holy Land. And who took part in it? Two kings and an old emperor led this crusade. They were Philip II of France, Richard I of England, and Frederick I of Germany.

Seal of Philip of France

Emperor Frederick was now almost seventy years of age, and he had been Germany's ruler for nearly forty years. His enemies called him Bar-ba-ros'sa, because of his long, red beard. We should think that he would have much preferred to remain at home and enjoy the quiet of his palace. But no, aged as he was, he liked adventure, and he sent a royal challenge to the great Mohammedan ruler, Sal'a-din. "Thou hast profaned the Holy Land," said the challenge, "and God willing, you shall learn by experience the might of our forces."

But Barbarossa never reached Jerusalem. He and his great army were not far from the Holy Land when they came to a river of pure water. It is said that while the old emperor was bathing in the stream, he was seized with cramps, and the swift current carried him away. The legend tells us that on a rock near the stream were carved the words, "Here the greatest of men shall perish." Even to this day there are German peasants who believe that Barbarossa is not dead, but that he is sleeping in a rocky cavern in the German hills, and that some day he will return to the people and help them.

Richard, known in history as the Lion-Hearted, was the first English king to engage in the crusades. But he had not sufficient money for the undertaking, and what did he do? He sold not only state positions, but church offices to any persons that could pay for them, no matter what their characters were. He gave towns more liberal charters if they paid him money. When one of his courtiers warned him against selling his castles and estates, he exclaimed, "I would sell London if I could find a purchaser rich enough to buy it."

Richard I
From an engraving by Vertue

Before Richard set out with his great army, he laid down the following laws:

"If a man slay his comrade on ship board, let him be bound to the dead man and cast into the sea."

"If a man slay his comrade on shore, let him be bound in the same way and be buried alive."

At last the crusaders were ready, and they started on their long journey. In the spring (1191) they reached Cy′prus, an island in the Med′i-ter-ra′ne-an

Sea, and from this place they set sail for the Holy Land. Finally they came to the harbor of A'cre, a town that the Christians were besieging. King Philip of France had already arrived there. The inhabitants were Turks. They had heard of the lion-hearted Richard, and they were indeed afraid of him.

Battle of Acre
From an old woodcut

But the Christians welcomed the arrival of the English king. "If you do not capture this town," he had said to his soldiers, "I will kill every one of you." It was a terrible siege, and Richard was always in the midst of the battle. More than two hundred thousand Christians and Mohammedans were killed, and the Turks were at last forced to surrender. Long after the siege of Acre the mere mention of King Richard's name brought terror to the inhabitants.

When the Turkish mothers desired their children to obey, they would say, "Be careful, or King Richard will get you." Or if a horse started at some object, the rider would call out, "Dost thou think that King Richard is behind it?"

King Philip was jealous of King Richard's fame. He complained of being ill and said that he would leave the crusade and return to France. "If you are ill, and are afraid to die in the Holy Land," said Richard scornfully, "I shall not urge you to remain, but it is a disgrace to turn back before the work is finished."

The French king, however, went back to France, and Richard was left alone in command. He then began his march toward Jerusalem. But all along the way he encountered the forces of Saladin, and terrible battles were fought. At As'ca-lon King Richard gave orders to rebuild the walls of the city that had been destroyed by the Mohammedans. The English king even carried mortar and stones himself, but the German Duke Le'o-pold refused to do such work. "I am a soldier, and not a carpenter or a mason," he said, and he returned to Germany.

There was an old chief of a tribe called As-sas'sins, who aided the Mohammedans. He was known as the "Old Man of the Mountain," and from his hiding-place he would send out the strongest of his men who would suddenly fall upon the Christians and stab them to death. And to-day we have the word "assassin," which comes from the name of this tribe.

Richard, too, had his equal in Saladin. The Mohammedan leader was as brave and as cruel as the

English king, but he was also generous. It is said that at one time on the march, when King Richard was suffering with a fever, Saladin sent him cooling fruits and ice from the mountain.

The crusaders had fought battles, they had captured cities, but they had not yet reached Jerusalem, although every night was heard in their camps the solemn cry, "Save the Holy Sepulcher!" But they were not permitted to take the Holy City, for Richard had unpleasant news, and he decided to return to England. His brother John was usurping his kingdom, the same John who afterward became king and was forced to sign the Magna Carta, as we saw in our last chapter. There was another disagreeable report — the king of France was plotting against Richard.

Richard slaughtering the Saracens
From an old print

He therefore proposed a three years' peace with Saladin, and it was granted. The Christians were permitted to enter Jerusalem and kneel at the Holy Sepulcher. But Richard would not even look at the Holy City. He veiled his face and exclaimed, "Those who are unwilling to rescue the Sepulcher of Christ are unworthy to view it."

It was not long before he returned to Europe. He knew he had enemies in Germany and France, and he disguised himself in the dress of a pilgrim. But in

Germany he was discovered by the ring on his finger, and Duke Leopold had his revenge, and cast him into prison.

There is a story told that King Richard's favorite minstrel, Blondel, journeyed from place to place in search of his master. He would sing a French song that he and the king had composed, for Richard was fond of music and poetry. One day, as he was singing the song outside of a German prison, he heard a voice from one of the windows humming the second stanza.

Richard's Prison Walls

"I have found the king," he said to himself, and he hastened to England to tell the glad news. The English were proud of their crusader king; they paid a large ransom for his freedom, and Richard returned to his people.

THE RESULTS OF THE CRUSADES

There were other expeditions to Jerusalem, and among them was a movement known as the Children's Crusade. It occurred in 1212. Boys and girls imitated their parents then as they do to-day. In France a young shepherd lad named Stephen preached a crusade, and many young people gathered to hear him.

Stephen was only twelve years of age. He told the boys and girls that Christ had visited him and had asked him to wear the cross and to lead the children to Jerusalem to recover the Holy Sepulcher. "God wills it! God wills it!" exclaimed the young people, and they went from town to town urging others to join them. "Where are you going?" they were asked.

Crusader Knights at Tilt

And the reply was, "We are going to Jerusalem." The children of Germany also joined the crusade, led by a youth named Nicholas. And there were more than fifty thousand boys and girls who set out on the journey, and as they marched they sang, "Lord Jesus, restore to us your Holy Cross."

But the young people did not reach the Holy City. Many of them died from hunger and thirst, from heat and fatigue. Others were taken on board ships and promised a free passage to the Holy Land; but they were deceived. The owners of the ships were slave merchants, and the children were sold as slaves.

THE RESULTS OF THE CRUSADES

The crusades covered a period of nearly two hundred years. But Jerusalem still remained in the power of the Mohammedans, and the Holy Sepulcher was not saved.

Notwithstanding the crusaders' failure to recover the Holy Land, much good came from these expeditions. They taught courtesy, honor, and justice. They aided the weak and protected the oppressed. They encouraged learning and travel. They gave ideas in regard to the customs of other countries. They extended trade and they developed commerce. Let us see how they did all this.

No city in Europe grew richer from trade with the East than did Venice in Italy. It is situated on the Ad'ri-at'ic Sea. It owned more than three thousand ships, and these were manned by more than forty thousand sailors. They would often carry the crusaders across the Mediterranean waters.

Venice, however, was more interested in trade than she was in recovering the Holy Sepulcher, and her ships would return with rich treasures from the faraway East. They would bring home spices, elegant silks, and beautiful mo-sa'ics. This trade not only introduced new articles of food and of clothing, but it gave the Venetians suggestions for adorning their public buildings and decorating their houses, and it was not long before the city became the home of merchant princes who lavished their wealth upon magnificent churches and palaces. Many articles that were brought from the East were now manufactured in Venice, and there sprang up inventions and new industries. As other people of Europe came to this city, they would carry back to their homes ideas and suggestions that they had received from the Venetians.

But there came a time when Venice had a rival in Genoa, another seaport of Italy. It was a stately port, and it well deserved the title "the proud." As it had also obtained important commercial privileges in the East, there were constant quarrels between Venice and Genoa, and it is said that wherever their ships met they fought.

The crusades not only incited trade and commerce, but they aroused the spirit of inquiry. They increased knowledge, and at the close of these expeditions the two great universities of England were established — Oxford (1200) and Cambridge (1229). The numerals that we use — 1, 2, 3, 4, 5, 6, 7, 8, 9, 0 — originated in India, and were introduced into Europe from Arabia in the twelfth century.

Five years before the last crusade, there was born in Florence the greatest of Italian poets — Dan'te (1265–1321). His grandfather had died in an expedition to Jerusalem. The poet said that he taught himself the art of bringing words into verse. His great poem, the "Divine Comedy," was prompted by his love for a little girl named Beatrice. Dante was only nine years of age when he first met her at a family festival, and she was but eight. Later Beatrice died and the poet revered her memory in his great poem.

Dante
From the portrait by Raphael

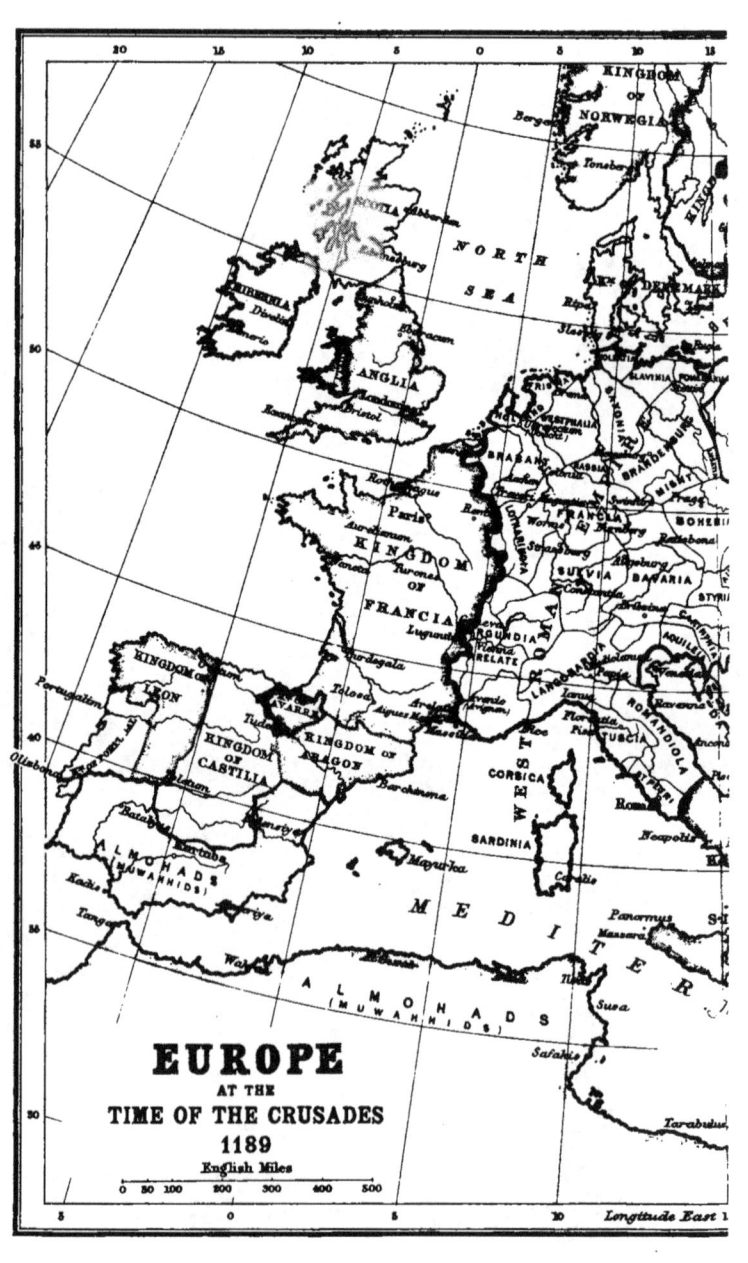

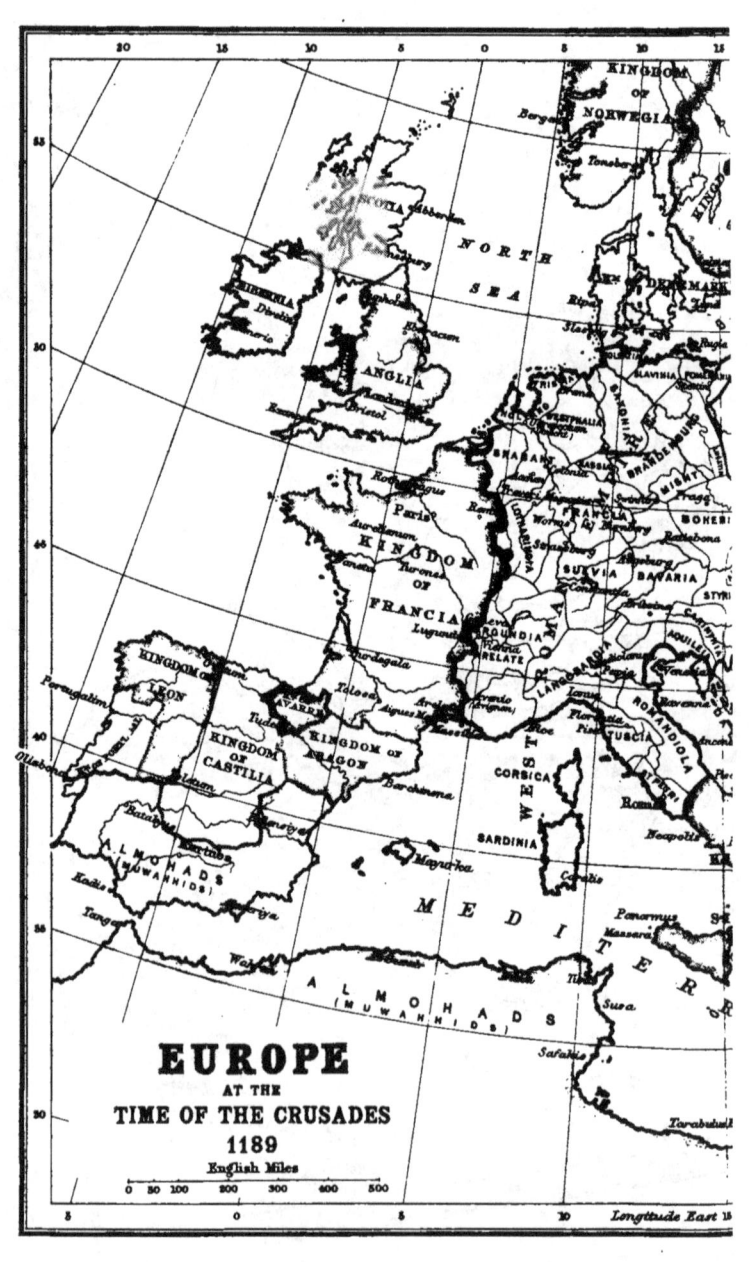

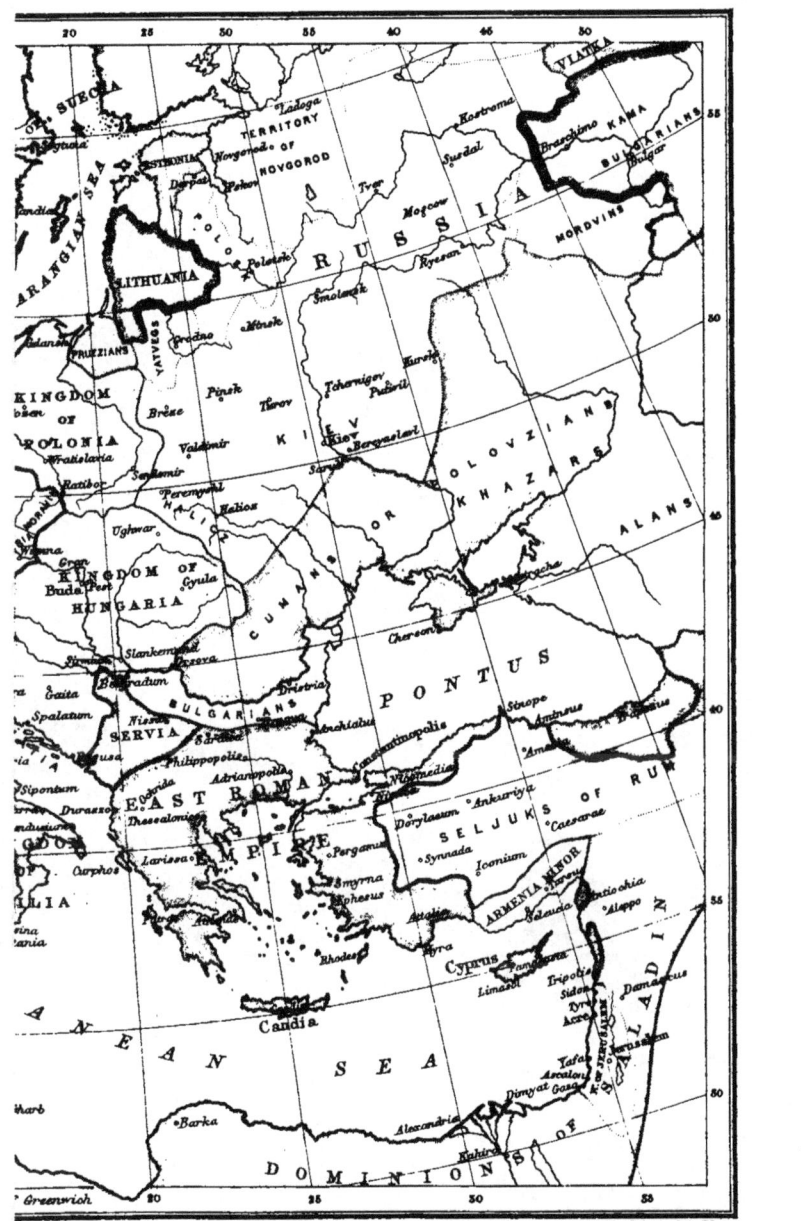

Before Dante died, Pe'trarch was born (1304–74). He was not only a great poet, but a scholar who did much to revive learning in Italy. His father desired that his son should become a lawyer, but young Petrarch found law distasteful. He much preferred to read the manuscripts of the great Roman poets. This made his father angry, and one day he threw the books into the fire; but the son pleaded so earnestly that the elder Petrarch allowed the half-burnt manuscripts to be rescued. Later Italy recognized the poet and scholar, and Rome crowned him with a wreath of laurel.

Petrarch
From the painting by Topanelli

At the close of the crusades, not only poetry, but sculpture and painting came into prominence. We see copies to-day of a famous painting of Dante by Giot'to. In his youth Giotto was a poor shepherd boy. He would often amuse himself, as he was tending his flock, by drawing pictures of the sheep with a piece of slate upon a stone. As he was one day thus engaged, a great painter named Ci'ma-bu'e saw him. "This boy will make an artist," said the painter, and he invited Giotto to his studio and gave him lessons.

Another good influence of the crusades was, that they caused persons of different rank to mingle with one another. And when the lord and the vassal returned home, there was a closer bond between them, for they had suffered together on the long march, and they had fought for the same purpose.

And, no doubt, out of the crusades came the system of chivalry, when the gallant gentleman put on his badge of knighthood and swore to speak the truth, to defend the right, and to protect the weak.

CHAPTER VIII

The Western World

THE people of Europe in the time of the crusades gave their attention to the East. They did not know of the great Western Continent which today is the home of the Americans. Old sagas (tales of the Northmen) tell us that before the time of the first crusade men from the Northland (Norway, Sweden, and Denmark) had reached that Western World. But they accomplished little, and there were very few people in Europe who knew the story of their voyages.

THE NORTHMEN

These hardy and daring Northmen loved the sea, and they were fond of its waves and storms. They would wander far from home in their rude dragon-shaped ships. They had no chart, no compass, but they had bold hearts and strong wills. They were, indeed, the true kings of the sea. They would often take a raven with them, a glossy black bird, and when they were far out on the waters, they would set the bird free. If it came back, they knew that no land was near, but if it did not return, these hardy sailors would row with all their might in the direction of the bird's flight.

At one time (about the year 860) some of these Northmen had sailed far, far out on the waters, and they were driven upon the shores of an island covered with ice. "We will call this land Iceland," they said, and by this name we know the island to-day. Later came other Northmen who settled on the island, and one of these settlers was Eric the Red. He had heard of an island west of Iceland, and he set out with a few followers in search of the land. They came to a craggy coast, but they soon found a grassy spot, and it afforded a contrast with its barren surroundings. "We will give this country an attractive name," said Eric, "and call it Greenland, for that will induce others to settle on the island." And it was not long before there was a colony of Northmen in Greenland.

Sending out Ravens to find Land

Eric had a son named Leif who had given up the worship of Thor (the Northmen's god) and had become a Christian. King Olaf of Norway sent Leif Ericson to Greenland to preach the story of the cross to the natives. Leif was as daring as his father, and he was glad for this opportunity. "Let us sail to the south," he said, "and see what the land there is like."

In the early fall (about the year 1000) he, with a crew of thirty-five hardy sailors, reached a stony and barren country which they called "Flat-Stone Land." It may have been Labrador. They went to their ship again and sailed southward. Again they cast anchor. This time they came to a wooded coast. "It shall be called Woodland," said Leif. This country was probably Nova Scotia.

But these Northmen wished to continue exploring. They followed the coast and came to a pleasant region where they decided to spend the winter. Here they cut down trees and built wooden huts. One evening a member of the party returned greatly excited. "I have found grape-vines and grapes," he said. And they gave the name Vinland (Wine-land) to the country. We do not know the exact spot of Vinland; it was, no doubt, somewhere between Nova Scotia and New York.

In the spring Leif returned to Greenland with his ship filled with timber. And since he was successful in his voyage, we know him through the old Norse stories as Leif the Lucky.

Other voyages were made to Vinland, but in time the Northmen were attacked by savage natives whom they called skrael'ings (an

Fragment of a Viking Ship found at Gokstadt

inferior people). Later a terrible plague, known as the Black Death, fell upon Norway, and one-third of its people died; and the voyages to the western world ceased.

These daring men from the North did not know that they had discovered a new continent. They were ignorant as to the shape of the earth, and they, no doubt, thought as they sailed out on the seas and came by accident to land, that they had reached only distant islands outside of their own country.

MARCO POLO

There lived in Venice about the middle of the thirteenth century a rich merchant named Nic'olo Polo. He and his brother started on a trading journey. They were fond of travel and they enjoyed new scenes. After many months they came to the great empire of Kublai Khan in eastern Asia. It is known to-day as China. Kublai Khan was delighted with these travelers. They told him about their own country, and when they were leaving, he asked them to return and bring with them one hundred teachers for his people.

A few years passed, but Nicolo Polo could not get men willing to go to this far-away land. At last he set out from Venice with his son Marco, a boy of seventeen years. They first went to Con-stan'ti-no'ple, and from this city they started on their long, long journey to China. They stopped at Acre and went to Jerusalem. "We will get holy oil from the lamp on the Sepulcher," said Nicolo Polo, "and take it to the great Khan."

Four years after leaving Venice they reached China. Marco was an observing youth and eager to learn the languages and customs of this strange people in the East; and before long Kublai Khan made him his private secretary. The emperor would send him on missions to distant provinces, and when the young man returned, he would greatly delight the Khan by describing the things that he had seen and the people that he had visited. "If Marco lives," said the emperor, "he will come to be a person of great worth."

Marco Polo

It was now twenty years since Nicolo Polo and his son left Venice, and the father becoming old was eager to return to his native city. It was not easy for them to say goodby to their kind friend, Kublai Khan. He gave them gold, precious stones, and beautiful silks as a parting gift, and the travelers were soon on their homeward way.

As Polo and his son had not returned, their friends at home said, "They are dead, they have been eaten up by some wild creatures." The people of Europe believed that the eastern coast of China ran off into a wild region of darkness where there were terrible monsters.

At last Marco Polo and his father were in Venice again, but even their own relatives and neighbors did not know these men in strange garments. And when the travelers told of their wonderful life in the East, the Venetians said, "These men are deceivers. Such things of which they tell cannot be true." Then what did the Polos do? They ripped open the seams in their long, coarse cloaks, and there fell out precious jewels — rubies, diamonds, and emeralds. When the people saw the rich treasures, they began to believe that the travelers' stories were true.

At this time Venice and Genoa were engaged in war, and Marco Polo had been home but a short time when he was made commander of a powerful galley. But he had the misfortune to be captured, and he was carried a prisoner to Genoa. In the prison he met another captive of the war who had been a writer, and Marco dictated to him the story of his wonderful travels. He told of the grandeur and wealth of the great Khan's empire. He spoke of an ocean east of China, and he gave accounts of a land which we know to-day as Japan.

As this book was written before the invention of printing, few at first had the opportunity to read it. Even these few readers said, "It is but an idle tale." And it took many years to prove that Marco Polo told the truth.

THE VOYAGE OF DIAZ

After the invention of printing, Polo's book was more widely read, and it became known in Portugal. In this country there lived Prince Henry, who was greatly interested in voyages to new lands. He established a school for navigators, and many scholars from

THE VOYAGE OF DIAZ

Italy who were tired of the petty wars between Genoa and Venice came to Portugal to study.

Men were trying to find an ocean route from Europe to the eastern shores of Asia. "Why not sail down the western coast of Africa?" some said, and the sailors of Portugal tried this. There were those who believed that the Indian Ocean connected with the Atlantic, and that ships could sail around Africa. But others said, "Asia extends to the east and Africa far to the south; and these two continents come together in the far southeast." Then there was the belief that no ship could enter the torrid zone without being swallowed up in some steaming whirlpool, or perishing in the face of mysterious, unknown dangers.

In 1486 Bar-thol'o-mew Diaz, a daring captain from Portugal, started on a voyage. He sailed south for many days without seeing land. He had passed the most southern point of Africa, but he did not know it. He then sailed toward the northeast and was in the Indian Ocean. He now wished to go farther, but his crew refused. They were tired of the voyage, and were eager to return to Portugal and the safety of familiar waters.

On their way home they came nearer to Africa, and they had great difficulty in passing the southern headland. "We will call it the Stormy Cape," Diaz said. But when he arrived in Portugal and described the cape to King John, his royal master said, "No, call it the Cape of Good Hope, for you may have found the ocean route to the wealth of the East."

CHRISTOPHER COLUMBUS

In 1453 the fierce and warlike Turks captured Constantinople, and then there was trouble for Genoa. Her merchants were returning with empty ships. "The Turks have refused to let us pass into the Black Sea," they said, "unless we pay a heavy tribute. If we do this all our profits will be lost." And so Genoa's rich trade with the East was given up, and her merchants became poor.

Columbus explaining his plans

Years later one of her citizens said, "We can reach India and China by sailing west across the Sea of Darkness" (the Atlantic). It was Christopher Columbus who said this. He put his plan before the learned men of his native city, but they laughed at him. And then what did he do? He went to Portugal. His brother Bartholomew had been with Diaz in his voyage around Africa, and this, no doubt, gave Columbus encouragement.

King John seemed to be much interested in what Columbus told him. But this king desired all the glory, and he secretly sent out a vessel to see whether the Italian's plan would be successful. The Portuguese ship sailed westward for some days, but it found no sign of a route to India. It then returned, and the captain and his crew laughed at the idea of reaching the East by sailing across the Sea of Darkness.

When Columbus heard what King John had done, he was angry, and left Portugal and went to Spain. But this country was engaged in war with the Moors, and the kingdom had little money for anything else.

Who were these Moors? They were Mohammedans from the northern coast of Africa. At the close of the eleventh century they invaded Spain, and in the southern part of the country they established their kingdom of Gra-na'da. They had a grand and beautiful palace called the Al-ham'bra. For several hundred years there were struggles between the Moors in the south and the Spaniards in the north.

Moorish costumes

Here is a story told of one of these battles. A brave Spanish knight had captured the rich Moorish city of Va-len'cia. He was known as the Cid, which means the chief. After a long life of adventure he became ill, and as he grew weaker each day he knew that he soon must die.

He ordered the gates of the city to be closed, and he then went to the church, where were assembled many knights and bishops. He said to them, "You know that I have never been conquered, and let not that happen to me at the end." He then called a bishop and four knights and told them what to do after his death. "The Moorish king will be here from Africa to besiege this city," he said. "Let not the Moors know that I have died. And when the king arrives, tell the people to go upon the walls and sound trumpets and to show the greatest joy that they can. For you certainly cannot keep the city after the enemy knows of my death."

Then he turned to a trusty knight and said, "Saddle my horse and arm him well. Clothe my body in armor and place it upon the horse so that it cannot fall off. And let a bishop go on one side, and you, my brave knight, on the other. Then march forth and fight with the Moorish king."

It was not long after this when the Cid died, and his followers did as they were directed. They left the city silently at midnight, led by five hundred knights bearing the banner of the Cid. When the Moorish king saw them he was dismayed. He quickly turned back and fled to the sea. And the city of the Cid was saved. "There were more than seventy thousand Christian knights," said one of the Moors as he described the Spaniards coming out to meet them. "And they were all as white as snow, and before them, mounted on a white horse, rode a knight of great size."

In 1492 the Moorish kingdom of Granada was seized by the Spaniards, and the keys of the Alhambra were given to the Spanish king Ferdinand. Would Spain now listen to Columbus? We shall see. Disappointed, he was about to leave the country, when the good prior Juan Perez told him not to be discouraged. "I have been Queen Isabella's religious adviser," he said, "and I will ask her to help you."

Not long after this the Queen sent money to Columbus so that he could buy clothes to appear well before her court. But now what happened? "If I am successful," said Columbus, "you must give me one-tenth of all the gold and other wealth that may be acquired." But Spain was not willing to accept such terms. Again Columbus went away

The Alhambra

discouraged. He had not gone far, however, when a royal messenger came after him in great haste, and bade him to return to court.

This time his terms were accepted, and on the third of August, 1492, the three little ships, the *Santa Maria*, the *Pinta*, and the *Niña*, set out from Pa'los on the great voyage. The king of Spain gave Columbus a letter to the Great Khan of China. There were one hundred and twenty men in the crew, and among them were criminals who had received pardon on their promise to go on the voyage. But Columbus had a better outfit than the daring Northmen. He had the mariner's compass which came from China. And he had the astrolabe, an instrument introduced by Prince Henry for observing the distance of stars; and by this instrument Columbus could find out his position.

After several weeks of sailing Columbus and his crew reached the Canary Islands. Here they cast anchor to mend the rudder of one ship and to change the sail of another. Again they set sail, and when they had sailed for several weeks, they saw a flock of land birds moving to the southwest, and these birds became their pilots.

Columbus

The ships sailed on and on, but no land was in sight. They had been on the waters for more than two months. The sailors begged Columbus to return, and when he refused, they secretly planned to throw him overboard. But now what happened? In the evening of October 10th a light was seen in the distance, and on the next morning there was the glad cry, "Land! land!"

On October 12th they went on shore, and Columbus and his men knelt and kissed the ground. Their eyes were filled with tears as they gave thanks to God. Then they planted the banner of Spain and took possession of the country in the name of King Ferdinand and Queen Isabella.

And what was this land? The natives called it Cat Island, but Columbus named it San Salvador (Holy

Saviour). He believed that he had reached India, and he called the natives Indians. The voyagers spent several months in the West Indies, and in January they were preparing to return to Spain with the glad news.

Only two of the vessels went back, as the *Santa Maria* had been shipwrecked. And on March 15th, 1493, the *Niña* and the *Pinta* sailed into the harbor of Palos.

Columbus made three other voyages to America. On the third voyage he reached the continent of South America, at the mouth of the Orinoco River.

A Spanish caravel
Sketch said to have been made by Columbus

But he did not know that he had discovered a new continent; he believed these strange coasts to be parts of Asia.

THE NAME AMERICA

And how did this continent come to be called America? It was named after A-mer'i-cus Ves-pu'ci-us, a friend of Columbus. He was born in Florence and had been employed by merchants who traded with the East. But when the Eastern trade was cut off, Vespucius left Florence and went to Spain. He made several voyages, and on one he reached the coast of

South America. He did not know that Columbus had been there before him.

When Vespucius returned home, he wrote to his friends in Florence telling of the wonderful new continent, of the delightful climate, and of the many strange animals that he had seen.

Americus Vespucius

A few years later a German teacher of geography wrote a little book in Latin. He had read the letters of Vespucius, and he suggested in his book that the new continent discovered should be called the land of Americus, or America. To this book he added translations into Latin of Vespucius' letters; and as Latin was the language common to all educated people in Europe, these letters were widely read, and the name America became popular.

In 1515, three years after the death of Vespucius, another German made a globe, and on this

Vespucius' autograph

globe the name America was given to South America only. But later it also became the name of the continent to the north.

JOHN CABOT

Before Columbus received the help of Spain, his brother Bartholomew had gone to England to ask King Henry VII for aid. But this monarch showed no interest in the project. Later Columbus returned from his voyage, and the news came to England that Spain's ships had reached India and the empire of the Great Khan.

This attracted the attention of John Cabot, an Italian who lived in Bristol, the principal seaport on the western coast of England. Merchants and seamen dwelt in this town; and more than one of their ships had ventured out some distance upon the Sea of Darkness.

John Cabot was born in Genoa, and he had been a merchant in Venice. He had traveled in Arabia, where he had bought spices from the caravans. "Where did you get these spices?" he would ask them, and they would reply, "From islands, far, far to the east."

Sebastian Cabot who accompanied his father John

And Cabot never forgot these spice islands. He believed the earth to be round. "By sailing west I can reach these islands," he said. But he was poor, and how was he to get a ship? King Henry aided him, and the people of Bristol were eager for the rich treasures of the East, and they fitted out a little vessel, named the *Matthew*, and the King gave him his royal commission. It was not long after this, on a beautiful May morning, 1497, that John Cabot, with a crew of eighteen men, sailed from the harbor of Bristol.

In June they reached land. How delighted they were. "We have found China," they said. They landed and planted a large cross with the banner of England. And Cabot did not forget Venice; he erected also the banner of Saint Mark — the patron saint of that city. They then began their search for the rich treasures of the East. They saw no people, nor did they find spices or gold. They found, however, some notched trees, snares for catching game, and needles for making nets. "People must live here," said Cabot.

He now decided to return to England, and by the end of July they were in Bristol again. They told of the part of China that they had visited. They spoke of the excellent climate. They said that the waters that washed its shores were filled with fish that could be caught not only with nets, but with baskets.

King Henry was pleased, and he clothed the discoverer in silk, and gave him ten pounds of English money ($48.66), and whenever Cabot appeared on the street, people followed him and called him the Great Admiral. Later he made a map of his discovery and a globe which greatly interested England.

But Cabot had not reached China. Just where he landed we do not know. It may have been Labrador or Cape Breton. There is no doubt, however, that he was the first white man, with the exception of the Northmen, to discover the mainland of North America.

VASCO DA GAMA

In the meantime Portugal was busy. Spain was not to be ahead of her. Diaz was successful in sailing around Africa. "We will send out another expedition," she said, "and this time we will reach India by way of Africa." With this aim in view she sent out Vas'co da Gama, and the parting instruction was, "Find for us the kingdom of Prester John."

This priest-king was supposed to have reigned over a rich and powerful kingdom somewhere in Central Asia. The legend said that twenty archbishops sat on his right hand, and that he was guarded by more than ten thousand knights, and that the commonest dishes on his table were of gold studded with precious jewels. Although Marco Polo had never seen this mysterious prince, he frequently mentioned him in his book, and there were many people in Europe in these early centuries who believed the story of Prester John.

On a hot July day, 1497, Da Gama sailed out on the waters from Portugal with three little vessels. Diaz had kept near the African coast; but not this daring Portuguese. Boldly he struck out upon the Sea of Darkness, and it was more than ninety days before he sighted land; in November he cast anchor near the Cape of Good Hope.

Vasco da Gama

Again he set sail, and it was with difficulty that his ships passed the Cape. This time they kept near the shore, and after they had gone some distance, they saw large elephants on the coast. Near an island were seals. "The big ones roared like lions," they said, "and the little ones cried like goats." And to-day this island is called Seal Island. They saw native negroes dancing on the beach, and Da Gama cast anchor and exchanged three bracelets for a large black ox.

In December they had passed the farthest point reached by Diaz. They sailed on until Christmas Day when they landed. They went on shore and called the place Natal after the day. They then struck out boldly across the Arabian Sea; and for more than twenty days no land was seen. But at length lofty mountains were sighted in the distance, and on a beautiful May day their dreams were realized — India had at last been reached by an ocean route.

A story tells us that the voyagers were graciously received by the Indian king who was reclining on a couch of green velvet. He gave them water to drink and bananas to eat. After many strange adventures in this country, they set sail for home, their ships laden with the riches of the East.

Portugal had found what Spain had been seeking; and when Da Gama returned with the rich treasures, there were people who made fun of Columbus. He had no gold to show or costly silks. They called him the Admiral of Mosquito Land who, instead of finding riches, had found a grave for the Spaniards.

BALBOA AND THE SOUTH SEA

After Columbus, other Spaniards came to the West Indies. Among them was Balboa. In Spain he had often been in debt, and he was not long in the New World when he made other debts. He was anxious to escape from his creditors, and an opportunity came. A relief ship was about to set sail for another colony, where some settlers were starving. Balboa found an empty barrel on the vessel, and he jumped into it. In a clever manner he closed the cask, leaving a little opening for air.

There he concealed himself until the vessel had gone some distance from shore. It was rather uncomfortable inside that barrel, and he was glad to get out of it. He now showed himself to the captain, who became so angry that he was about to throw the debtor overboard; but the tall, handsome figure of Balboa moved him to pity, and he allowed him to remain.

Balboa taken aboard ship

Later Balboa with some followers reached the Isthmus of Panama. They were seeking for riches. After going from one Indian village to another, they came to a friendly chief who gave them gold trinkets. And as the Spaniards were dividing the treasures, they quarreled among themselves. When the Indian chief saw how eager they were for gold, he pointed to a distant mountain range, saying, "Beyond that is a great body of water on whose shore is a land filled with gold."

Balboa and his two hundred followers set out, determined now not only to seek for gold, but to find an ocean for Spain, for then their reward would be great. On they went, through thick forests and over rocky hills. At last they came to a mountain from whose summit they saw the great expanse of water. They descended on the western side, and Balboa took possession of the vast sea in the name of Spain. This was in the year 1513. He called it the South Sea, but to-day we know it as the Pacific Ocean.

MAGELLAN'S VOYAGE

This great body of water was named the Pacific Ocean by Ferdinand Ma-gel'lan.

Magellan was born in Portugal. When a youth he served as a page in the king's court at Lisbon. Later he sailed for India by way of Africa, and he remained in the East seven years.

Magellan

People were beginning to see that a new world lay between Europe and Asia. Magellan believed that if he could find a channel through this land, he could then sail across the ocean discovered by Balboa, and thus reach the spice islands by sailing west. He told his plan to the king of Portugal, but the king laughed at such "a crazy idea," and refused to help him. Then Magellan did what Columbus had done. He left Portugal and went to Spain.

King Charles of Spain was much interested in his plan. He believed that such a route was possible; and late in September, 1519, Magellan left Spain with a fleet of five vessels. This made the king of Portugal angry, and he said, "Such actions are those of a traitor." It is true this king had refused to give help; but he now secretly feared that Magellan might reach the spice islands, and Spain, and not Portugal, would have the glory.

Magellan's fleet sailed down the African coast, and it was not long before they reached the Cape Verde Islands. They continued to sail southwest, and in November they came to the coast of Brazil. Two months after this they entered the mouth of a great river, known to-day as the Ri'o de la Pla'ta. "This is the channel for which we have been looking," said Magellan, and the men were happy. They sailed up the stream — but now what happened? They found that the water was fresh. And as they returned to the coast, the crew began to grumble and were eager to go back to Spain.

Around the world

The weather was cold and the storms were severe; but there were other hardships. Food was becoming scarce and the ration was less each day. "Why should we perish here in the cold?" asked the sailors. "Instead of reaching the spice islands, we shall land on some icy shore." But Magellan would not turn back. "You are Spaniards," he said, "and have you not the pride of your country? Be patient, we shall reach the passage in the spring, and King Charles will reward you well. It would show weakness to give up the undertaking now." He thus quieted the crew for a time. But at length they again complained. This time, however, Magellan was compelled to be severe, and there was bloodshed. After that his authority was not questioned.

Thirteen months had passed since they had left Spain. It was now October, and again they were entering a channel. At last they found the passage that they were seeking. Day after day they sailed and finally reached an ocean. Its waters seemed calm after their stormy voyage, and Magellan said, "Let us name it the Pacific Ocean." And the passage through which they sailed, off the southern coast of South America, is known to-day as the Straits of Magellan.

But the voyage was by no means ended. If they sailed back by the way they came, they would starve. They had now but three ships — one was wrecked and another had deserted. They decided to sail across the Pacific Ocean in the hope that land would soon be reached and food could be obtained. But it was more than three months before they sighted land, and then they reached a group of islands. The inhabitants brought them oranges, bananas, and cocoanuts; but these natives stole from the Spanish ships whatever they could lay hands on, and Magellan named the islands the Ladrones (which means "robbers").

Again they set sail, and later they came to another group of islands which they called the Philippines, after the king's son Philip. The king of one of the islands became a Christian. He ordered the idols to be burned and a cross to be erected, and he and his people were baptized. But a chief of a neighboring island refused to pay homage to the Christian king, and then there was war, and in the desperate fight Magellan was killed.

Magellan had reached the spice islands, but only one ship remained — the *Victoria*. Not only the brave leader was killed, but many of the crew had died from sickness. Those who were left sailed south to the Mo-luc'cas, and from these islands the *Victoria* took on board twenty-six tons of cloves. She then crossed the Indian Ocean and sailed around Africa.

And three years after the fleet had set out, the *Victoria* was again in Spain. At last Asia was reached by sailing west, and the first great voyage around the world proved that the earth is round.

JACQUES CARTIER

France was also looking for a western route to China, and in April, 1534, Cartier' left St. Malo with two little ships and sailed straight across the ocean. In May he sighted New'found-land, and here he saw floating ice and white bears. Fishermen had been here as early as 1504, and had been coming ever since to the banks of Newfoundland for codfish. They had not explored the mainland, for they were interested only in fishing.

Jacques Cartier

But Cartier came for an entirely different purpose. The Spaniards were giving their attention to the south.

"There must be a northwest passage to the sea which leads to China," said Cartier. And this northwest passage he was seeking.

He and his little party explored the coast of Newfoundland. They met some Indians who seemed friendly. Cartier and his men cut down a large tree, and from it they made a cross thirty feet high, on which were carved the words, "Long live the King." They then erected the cross and knelt down before it giving thanks to God, and they thus took possession of the country in the name of the king of France.

But the Indians did not like the planting of the cross. An old chief clad in bearskin, with several of his braves, approached the Frenchmen, and made signs that Cartier understood to mean, "This is our country, and you must not set up any more crosses." The explorers deceived the Indians. They said that the cross was only a light to guide other men who might come to these shores. And when they gave the Indians red caps and copper chains, the old chief promised not to destroy the cross.

Winter was coming on, and the Frenchmen returned to France telling of what they had seen — icebergs, white bears, and red men who lived by fishing and hunting. The next year the king gave Cartier three vessels to find out more about this new country, to establish trading posts with the Indians, and above all, to seek a northwest passage to China.

Again they sailed straight across the ocean. They entered a great gulf into which flowed a broad river. Cartier called the river the St. Lawrence, as he had discovered it on St. Lawrence's day, and the gulf came to be known as the Gulf of St. Lawrence. The water of the river was fresh, and the stream became narrower the farther they went. "But even fresh water may lead to the sea that touches the shores of China," said Cartier.

They sailed up the river and came to a great cliff that extended out into the water, and there on the rock dwelt an old Indian chief with his tribe. He welcomed the Frenchmen, and gave them bearskins in exchange for knives and red beads. But when the explorers started to go farther up the river, the old chief objected, and he ordered three of his braves to put on black and white dogskins, to besmear their faces as black as coal, and to wear long horns on their heads.

When the Frenchmen saw these strangely dressed

Cartier taking possession in the name of France

beings approaching in a canoe, they wondered who they were. "The chief says they are messengers of the Great Spirit," said the Indian interpreter, "who dwells up the river and who does not like pale-faced men." But Cartier only laughed at this, and he and his men sailed on farther up the stream.

In the days of this old Indian chief there stood on

the cliff only a few Indian wigwams, but to-day there stands on this great rock the quaint city of Quebec.

It was now early autumn. The explorers were passing thickly wooded shores, and the foliage was rich in red and yellow. They finally reached an island, and there they found an Indian village at the foot of a beautiful mount.

In the village were fifty cabins built of wood and covered over with bark and skins. Each cabin had a garret where the Indian kept his corn to make bread. He would beat the corn into powder with wooden hammers, and then he would make a paste, and cut it into cakes. These cakes he would lay between hot stones, and in this way the Indian baked his corn bread.

Around the village were three palisades of strong stakes to protect it from attack. The Frenchmen ascended the mount beyond, and the view was so beautiful that Cartier exclaimed, "This is, indeed, Mount Royal," and later the Indian village became the site of a French town which we know as Montreal.

The explorers then returned to their camp farther down the river where they spent the winter. They were anxious for this season to be past, for they had never experienced such cold weather, and many of their number died. The ground was so frozen that no graves could be dug, and the bodies were buried in snowdrifts.

But in the spring when the ice melted and the ships could sail out of the river, Cartier and his party returned to France. He had not found a northwest

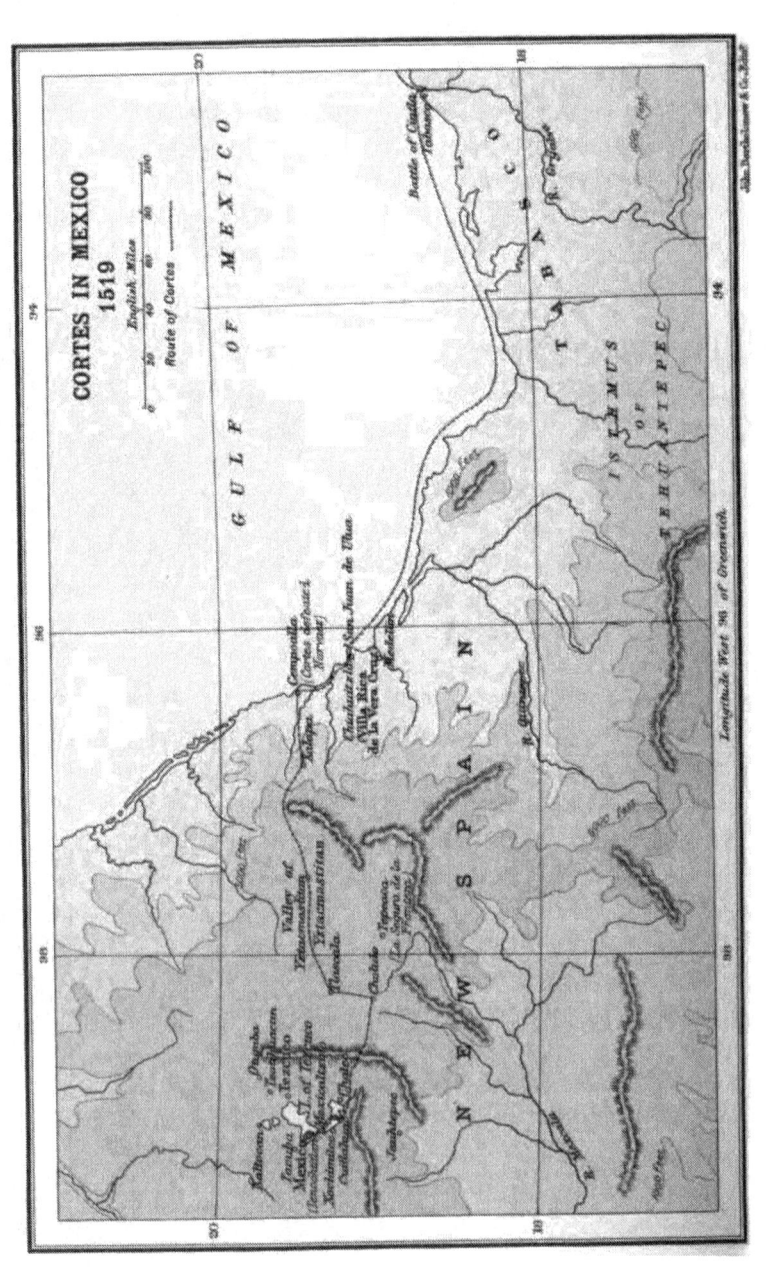

passage, but he had met Indians who exchanged rich furs for cheap colored beads, and he had discovered a great river — the St. Lawrence.

CORTEZ AND MEXICO

After Balboa discovered the Pacific Ocean there were other Spaniards in the West Indies who were eager to find the land of gold. A Spanish exploring party had returned from the Mexican coast with rich treasures — jewels and gold ornaments, which the natives readily exchanged for glass beads, as they had never seen glass before. They told the explorers of a wonderful city in the interior ruled by a mighty king who had no end of gold. "This must be the kingdom of the great Khan," said the Spaniards. But they soon encountered hostile Indians, and the explorers thought it wise to turn back.

When they arrived in Cuba, they told of the wonderful things that they had seen and heard, and the governor of the island decided to send out another expedition to explore the land of the rich and powerful king. There was no one more fitted to command than Her-nan'do Cortez. He was not only noted for his bravery and power of endurance, but he was bold and crafty.

Accordingly, in February, 1519, Cortez started out with eleven vessels bearing more than six hundred Spaniards. He also took with him two hundred Indians, sixteen horses, and fourteen cannon. And early in March he landed on the coast of Yu-ca-tan', a peninsula in the eastern part of Mexico. Later he came within the empire of the great Montezuma, the king of the Aztecs. Their capital was Mexico, named after the war-god.

It is believed that these people came from the north. They wandered from place to place until they reached a lake. The legend tells us that as the sun arose, the Aztecs saw a great eagle perched upon a cactus that was growing out of a rock, and its wings were spread toward the rising sun. The bird held a large serpent in its claws. "This is a favorable sign," said the people, "and here by the lake we will build our city." Even to this day the eagle and the cactus form the emblems of the Mexican republic.

The emblem of Mexico

The story also relates that the great god of the air once dwelt upon earth; and while he was with the people, they had peace and prosperity. But other gods compelled him to leave the country, and he then sailed away in his magic boat. Before he left, however, he told the people that a day would come when he would return to them. And when they heard of the wonderful strangers in their land, they began to think that probably their kind god had come back.

The Spaniards were soon cutting down bushes, and the natives were helping them to build huts with stakes and earth. One day they were visited by an ambassador sent by Montezuma. He asked the strangers about their country and why they came to Mexico. "I am the subject of a powerful king beyond the seas," said Cortez, "and he has sent me with a present to your king, and a message that I must deliver in person."

But the Aztecs wondered whether there could be another king as mighty as Montezuma. This monarch feared that the Spaniards meant harm to his country, so he had sent with the messenger a present to gain the stranger's good-will. The gift consisted of a great basket of golden ornaments, cloaks of curious feather-work, and ten loads of fine cotton. "The stories that we have heard about the wealth of this king are indeed true," said the Spaniards.

Hernando Cortez
From an old effigy

The Aztecs had never seen horses, and when Cortez ordered the riders to go through exercises, the natives were astonished. They thought that the rider and horse were one animal. But they were more alarmed when a cannon was fired, when they saw its smoke and flame, and beheld what the cannon shot could do. The natives allowed nothing to escape their notice. The Aztecs were Indians. They used picture-writing, and the ambassador's attendants were busily making pictures of what they had seen to take back to their king.

When the messengers returned, Montezuma was indeed frightened. He sent another present to Cortez and asked him to leave the shores and not to enter the Mexican capital. But since the Spaniard had received the gifts, he was more determined than ever to march on to the city.

Cortez approaching the Aztec city

The capital was built on an island in a salt lake. Three causeways of solid masonry led to it from the mainland. The houses of the city were large and built of stone coated over with white stucco. The flat roofs were often covered with flower-gardens.

The great temple stood in the center of the capital, surrounded by a stone wall which was entered by four gateways.

Now the Spaniards had reached the city, and Montezuma, borne on a litter, came out to meet them. Over his shoulders was thrown a cloak of the finest cotton studded with pearls and emeralds. On his head was the royal plume of green feathers, and on his feet were sandals with soles of gold. He appointed his brother to conduct the strangers to a large building near the temple, and this was to be their quarters.

The Spaniards had not been in the city long when the Aztecs said, "They are not gods. They have come to rob us. They throw down our idols and put up their crosses." And not many months passed before there was a desperate fight. Montezuma was taken prisoner, and the city of Mexico fell into the hands of the Spaniards.

Cortez had won for Spain an empire of great wealth. The natives were converted to Christianity and gradually Spanish was the language spoken. Spain governed Mexico until the nineteenth century, when it became a republic. Porfirio Diaz became president in 1884, and remained at the head of the government until 1911, when civil war broke out in the country, and he and his party were forced to surrender to the revolutionists.

A modern Mexican cavalryman

THE SEARCH FOR GOLD

It was hardly five years after Cortez had conquered Mexico, when Pi-zar′ro, another Spaniard, left the Isthmus of Panama in a little ship with a crew of eighty men. They had heard that to the south was a rich kingdom of gold.

They sailed along the South American coast until they came to Peru; and here they entered a city the walls of whose temples were lined with gold. They made friends with the natives and learned all they could about the people. They then returned to Panama with rich treasures of gold and silver.

Pizarro on shipboard

But Pizarro was not satisfied with a mere visit to the country. As Cortez had conquered Mexico, he would conquer Peru. And not five years passed before the Spaniard again set sail for the rich kingdom in the south. This time he had three hundred men and more than fifty horses.

News soon reached the ruler of Peru, who was called the Inca, that strangers had arrived on his shore. Like the Aztecs the Peruvians had never seen horses before; and the Inca thought it wise to make friends with a people that had such strange animals. Accordingly when he met the Spaniards he received them with great splendor. Pizarro invited him to his tent, and it was not long before the Indian chief called upon the strangers with a large number of attendants.

"Now is our opportunity," said Pizarro, "and we

must act quickly. At a signal a gun was fired and the horses with their riders rushed forward, and the Peruvians fled in terror. They thought the Spaniards must be gods, their horses monsters of the sea, and their firearms thunderbolts from the sky.

But the Inca did not escape, he was taken prisoner. However, he was promised his freedom if he would give Pizarro a great quantity of gold and silver. To raise this ransom the Peruvians stripped their temples and palaces of treasures; and the people brought gold to the value of millions of dollars to the Spaniards. Now Pizarro had his gold but he did not keep his promise and release the Inca. The Indian monarch was shamefully put to death, and Spain won another rich empire.

Ferdinand De Soto was with Pizarro in his conquest of Peru, and as his share of the spoils he received gold and silver to the value of many thousands of dollars. And now, after many years of adventure in the new world, De Soto returned to Spain a rich man. But he was not there long when a Spaniard came back from America with the wonderful story of El Do-ra'do — the Gilded Man. "We must find the kingdom of the Gilded Chieftain," said De Soto and he again set sail for the New World.

The legend tells us that on the top of a little mountain was a lake in which an Indian goddess dwelt. And whenever a certain tribe chose a new monarch, they would march to this lake with the chief borne on a litter from which hung sheets of gold. He was, indeed, the Gilded Man, for his body had been smeared with gum and over this was spread a layer of gold dust. When he reached the lake he plunged into the water to wash off the covering of gold; and the other warriors threw into the lake golden ornaments and precious jewels. Then the musicians played upon the horns and pipes, and the Indians danced on the water's edge. By this ceremony the red men believed that they would gain the favor of the goddess of the lake.

In this search for more gold De Soto first went to Cuba and from that island he set sail for Florida. He had with him six hundred men and more than two hundred horses. After landing they began their march, but the kingdom of the Gilded Man was nowhere in sight. On and on the Spaniards went through the pathless woods, through thick underbrush and swampy ground; and more than once they met unfriendly Indians who shot at them with bows and arrows from behind trees.

De Soto on the March

They were marching toward the northeast, and they finally came to a river which we know as the Savannah. On the opposite side of the stream was an Indian village, and here lived a young queen. The Spaniards made friends with the tribe, and the queen was rowed across the waters to meet De Soto. She placed on his neck a string of beautiful pearls to show that her people would be friendly toward the strangers and De Soto gave her a handsome gold ring in return.

But the Spaniards found no gold here, and again they were on their march. They went west, then south, and finally north, crossing what is now known as the states of Georgia, Alabama, and Mississippi. They endured many hardships, they suffered hunger and sickness, and as they went on, their numbers were becoming less, but they were determined to find gold. Even their clothes turned to rags and they were forced to dress in the skins of wild animals.

Three years had passed since they started out in search for El Dorado; but De Soto would not turn back. On they went and now they came to the banks of a long and wonderful river. "This is, indeed, the Father of Waters of which we have heard the Indians tell," said De Soto. Then they cut down trees and built boats, and rowed across the great stream.

They continued their march westward, but they found no gilded city. They then turned south and came to the banks of the Great River again. And as De Soto was planning to build a large boat to sail down the river to the Gulf of Mexico, and then back to Cuba, he became ill with fever and died; and his followers lowered his body in the great Father of Waters.

De Soto did not find the city of the Gilded Man, but he discovered a great river (1541), which is known to-day as the Mississippi.

CHAPTER IX

European Claims to America

The white banner of Columbus (F and Y for Ferdinand and Ysabel)

SINCE Spain had conquered Mexico and Peru, and Spanish ships were bringing home rich treasures, other nations of Europe were eager to find gold and silver. Indeed it was necessary for Spain to be watchful or her rich treasure ships would be captured, and there was no country more eager to capture them than England.

There had been a bitter feeling between these two countries ever since Elizabeth ascended the English throne in 1558. In the beginning of the sixteenth century the church of England was the Roman Catholic Church, but Elizabeth was a Protestant and the state church had become Protestant. Philip II, king of Spain, was a strong champion of the Catholic Church, and he called the English heretics — those who choose their own belief instead of the belief of the Church.

The quarrels between Spain and England continued, and besides differences in religion, there was more reason for bitter feeling. Since the days of Diaz, Portugal was engaged in African slave-trade. Now

English vessels were going to Africa for negroes. They would take their captives on board, and then sail on to the West Indies or South America. The Spanish planters and miners were in need of cheap labor, and they were only too eager to exchange sugar, gold, and pearls for slaves.

Some of these English ships were commanded by Captain John Hawkins, one of the bravest of seamen. At one time, when he was returning with his little squadron of five vessels to England, a storm arose and he was compelled to seek shelter in a Spanish port where there were ships loaded with rich treasures.

Soon afterward a fleet of thirteen vessels from Spain arrived in the harbor, and then there was trouble. "We shall not interfere with your ships, if you will let us remain in this port to repair our vessel," said Captain Hawkins to the Spanish admiral. It was agreed, but the agreement had no sooner been made than the English ships were suddenly attacked by the Spaniards, and after a desperate fight three of Captain Hawkins's vessels were destroyed. He then

A Spanish treasure ship

returned to England vowing vengeance on the treacherous Spaniards.

SIR FRANCIS DRAKE

There was no one more eager to punish the Spaniards than Francis Drake, another valiant seaman. He was with Captain Hawkins on the voyage when the English ships were attacked. Now he was planning to sail on the Pacific Ocean where he could seize the enemies' vessels as they came out of the harbors of Mexico and Peru with their rich treasures.

An Englishman of 1633

Queen Elizabeth was, indeed, proud of this daring rover of the sea, and she gladly consented to fit out a fleet for him. England was prosperous now and the queen knew only too well that a handsomely furnished ship would reflect credit on her country.

The Spaniards had once said, "The English have houses made of sticks and dirt." But they had no reason to say that in Elizabeth's time. The prosperity and the wealth of the country were seen in the beautiful houses that were built and in the increase of daily comforts.

The peasant now had a feather-bed and a pillow instead of straw and a round log. He had pewter and tin dishes on his cupboard in place of the wooden ones. And the house of the nobleman was richly furnished and decorated with tapestries of silk and silver. He had glass from Venice on his table, and china dishes were beginning to be seen. It is true that in the early part of the sixteenth century he used his fingers in the place of a knife and fork, but before the century closed he had the knife. He waited, however, a little longer for the fork, for that did not come into use before 1611.

Queen Elizabeth liked splendor, and nowhere was this more evident than in the richness of her dress. It is said that she left at her death three thousand gowns made from the most costly material.

She saw that nothing was undone when she fitted out the flag-ship of Francis Drake — the *Pelican*. There were gold and silver dishes on the table in the cabin, and strains of music made merriment for the voyagers as the fleet of five vessels sailed proudly out of Plymouth harbor one November day, 1577. There were one hundred and fifty men in the crew and fourteen boys.

An English lady of 1631

They kept their plans a secret, for it would not be wise to let the Spaniards know the object of their voyage. "We will deceive them by sailing to Africa," said Drake. And on they sailed to the African coast, then southwest, and it was not long before they came to Brazil, in South America.

It was not a smooth voyage; they encountered fierce

Queen Elizabeth knighting Drake on board the *Golden Hind* at Depford, April 4, 1581. From the painting by Sir John Gilbert, R. A.

storms, and now only the flag-ship was left to sail through the Straits of Magellan, and the name of the ship was changed from the *Pelican* to the *Golden Hind*.

Soon the *Golden Hind* was out on the Pacific where Spain was mistress of the sea. It was a bold undertaking, indeed, for an English ship to show itself on these waters. Not many weeks passed before Drake saw in the distance the object of his search — a Spanish ship. Nearer and nearer the two ships approached and the captain of the *Golden Hind* soon saw that the enemy's vessel was the *Spitfire*, a treasure ship with a rich cargo.

The English, however, were masters of the situation; the Spaniards soon came to terms, and the cargo of rich treasures was transferred to Drake and his crew. Now that they had the prize the sailors of the *Golden Hind* were eager to return home. But their commander said, "We dare not go back the way we came. The enemy will be after us."

And what did they do? They crossed the Pacific Ocean to the Philippine Islands, and then they sailed on the Indian Ocean. Soon they passed the Cape of Good Hope, and along the coast of Africa they went.

It was nearly four years since Drake had set sail from England, and now he was in the harbor of Plymouth again.

Queen Elizabeth was not only delighted with the jewels and gold brought home, but she was proud of the sailor who was the first Englishman to sail around the world. She went on board the *Golden Hind*, and there on the deck of the little ship she knighted its commander, and he was now the great admiral-at-sea — Sir Francis Drake.

THE GENTLE LORD DE BAYARD

Spain had another rival — France. These two countries were engaged in war; both were fighting for the rule of Italy. Spain was occupying Naples; and the French, Milan. But after a short war the Spaniards took Milan.

A handsome young prince, only twenty years of age, now became king of France. He is known as Francis I. Not many weeks passed after his coronation when the young king made preparations to get back Milan, and he had a brave knight to help him — Lord de Bayard.

Bayard was born of a noble family. He had served as a page to a French duke. Later, his handsome face, his pleasing manner, his skill in the tilt attracted the French king, Charles VIII, who took him to Italy; and in a short time young Bayard captured a standard in battle. The king then knighted him, and he was known as Lord de Bayard.

Cannon used in Bayard's campaigns

When Francis came to the throne Lord de Bayard had served some years in the Italian wars, and he had become famous for his ability and his daring deeds. On one occasion, it is said, that single-handed he defended a bridge against two hundred Spaniards.

And now, when war again broke out between the king of France and the king of Spain, Bayard defended a frontier town with only one thousand men against an army of thirty-five thousand. This resistance saved central France from being invaded by the enemy, and the brave knight was declared to be the savior of his country.

Later the French again occupied Milan. Bayard was now asked to save another French army in Italy. A battle occurred and the knight was mortally wounded. He desired to be placed against a tree so that he might die facing the enemy. An officer of the Spanish army came up to the dying man and expressed sympathy. This officer had deserted the French and had joined the Spaniards, and Bayard refused his sympathy. "My lord, I thank you," he said, "but pity is not for me who dies a true man, serving my king; pity is for you who bears arms against your prince, your country, and your oath."

Even the enemy admired the noble Bayard for his virtues. They laid him on a camp-bed and placed a tent over him, and not three hours passed when the knight died praying, "Father, I beseech Thee not to look upon the faults that I have committed." In the words of his secretary, "The gentle Lord de Bayard loved and feared God, and he never swerved from speaking the truth." And in history we know him as "the knight without fear and without reproach."

It was in the year 1524 that he died, and in that same year the French were defeated in Italy, and again they lost Milan.

THE FATE OF FORT CAROLINA

It was in the reign of Francis I that Cartier had discovered the St. Lawrence River; but an attempt to establish a colony on that river had failed, and nothing more was done for some time. France was too busy at home; she had her war with Spain and the Protestants, too, were causing trouble.

In the early centuries the pope at Rome was considered the head of all the Christian churches except the Greek Catholic Church in Russia and in Greece. The word "catholic" comes from two Greek words meaning entirely, whole, hence pertaining to the whole Christian Church. As soon as Spain laid claim to the New World she had her title confirmed by the pope. Portugal did the same. As early as 1493 the pope had divided the world into two portions by drawing a line on his map from north to south out in the Atlantic Ocean. Portugal could claim any land that she might discover east of this line; while Spain had the right to the land west of it.

Nearly thirty years had passed since Cartier had ascended the St. Lawrence River, and now King Henry II of France was eager to have a portion of America. And when Admiral Coligny (Co-li-nyi') asked him to fit out vessels to carry emigrants to the New World, the king readily agreed.

Henry was a Roman Catholic and he disliked the

Protestants, or Hu'gue-nots as they were called, in France. Coligny was a Protestant, and his great desire was to found a settlement in America where the Huguenots would not be persecuted as they were in France. But he deemed it not wise to tell the king this; it was better for Henry to think that the object of the expedition was for France rather than for religion.

Admiral Coligny

At length two French vessels set out with emigrants who were mostly Protestants. After sailing for more than three months they came to the coast of Brazil. They landed and called the place Fort Coligny after their friend in France. But they were soon attacked by the Portuguese and the expedition ended in failure.

When the king learned that Coligny's real object was to found a colony for the Protestants, he began to think that it was a good idea to rid the country of the Huguenots, as they were becoming a strong political party in France. Accordingly another expedition was sent out. This time the emigrants landed in Florida at the mouth of a great river; as it was the first of May they called the stream the River of May, but we know it to-day as the Saint John's. Again there was failure.

Now two years had passed since the first expedition had set out, and another attempt was made to establish a colony in Florida. Again the River of May was reached. A fort was built and named Carolina in honor of Charles IX, now king of France. There were not only attacks by the Indians but the people were not fitted to endure the hardships in a land of swamps and pine forests. They were discontented and they suffered from hunger. They were about to give up when a French fleet arrived in the harbor with supplies. Now they were happy, and they would set to work and begin life anew. But something else happened.

A ship had sailed from Spain under Me-nen'-dez with a commission to conquer Florida. The Spaniards finally reached a small stream, which they called St. Augustine, and here they landed and planted the cross. This was in 1565, and it marked the beginning of the oldest town in the United States — St. Augustine in Florida.

Old Gateway at St. Augustine

They had heard of the French at Fort Carolina and Menendez decided to attack the Protestant colony. "This is the Church's war," he said, "and it must be fought with blood and fire." The Spaniards surprised the French one dark night. They rushed in upon them shouting their battle-cry, "Santiago! Santiago!" (Saint Iago), and the fort was soon taken. This was the last attempt on the part of the French to establish a colony in Florida.

SPAIN AND THE DUTCH

Now Spain had trouble with her subjects, the Dutch. The Dutch have always been known as a plucky people. Indeed, they had earned the right to their country, for they had taken much of the land from the sea. At low tide they would build walls of stone as far out from the shore as they could. The walls were called dikes and the sea could not climb over these embankments. Their country was well named Netherlands (lowlands) and we know it to-day as Holland (from two words hollow and land).

A Windmill in Holland

The Dutch must still fight the sea. They build their dikes of earth and clay, and these embankments extend not only along the seacoast for many miles but also into the interior of the country, for the people realize that at any time rivers and lakes may flood their land. The dikes are broad. On them are driveways, rows of beautiful trees, and fine buildings. And we cannot picture Holland without its windmills. They not only pump the water into the canals and drain the land, but they grind the corn and saw the wood. Indeed, this land of the Dutch is well called the country of dikes and windmills.

Philip II was not only the king of Spain but he was

ruler of the Netherlands. He had no sooner come to power than he was determined to punish the heretics, the Protestants, in the Dutch provinces. And what did he do?

He sent Spanish soldiers into the country, who lived at free quarters on the inhabitants. He declared that the Protestants should not hold any meetings, and if they disobeyed they were to be punished.

A Street in Holland

He appointed his half-sister, the Duchess of Par'ma, as regent, and he also had a council of state to carry out his laws while he was in Spain. The Dutch were not only a sturdy people but they were independent and they rebelled against such laws as Philip made. Three hundred nobles, Catholics as well as Protestants, assembled one day and drew up a petition setting forth their grievances. They then marched four abreast to the court of the regent.

They were not dressed as noblemen, they did not wear their cloaks of silk and velvet and their decorations of gold. They did not carry arms, and they

were not mounted on horses. As they approached
the court of the regent, a courtier whispered to the
duchess, "Do not fear, it is only a company of
beggars." Later at a dinner where the nobles were
assembled one of their number filled a wooden bowl
with wine and drank the health of the "beggars."
And the term became another name for the friends
of Dutch liberty, and their party cry was "Long live
the beggars!" They put on the beggar's dress — a
cloak of coarse cloth — and they wore as a symbol a
little wooden bowl on the cap.

The duchess received the noblemen graciously and
she sent a messenger to the king with their petition.

WILLIAM OF ORANGE

There was a member of the council who disliked to
see the people treated so unjustly. He was a handsome young nobleman, not thirty years of age. We
know him as William of Orange. He was so called
because he had inherited the French province of
Orange. William resigned his seat in the council,
and now he began working on a plan to restore peace
and freedom to the country. He was a wealthy
prince and he had many friends. His generous nature
and his tact won the good-will of the people. He
gained the title of William the Silent. It was difficult
even for his friends to read his thoughts if he deemed
it wise to be on his guard.

King Philip had received the petition, but instead
of granting the request he dismissed the duchess and
he appointed the Duke of Alva to succeed her. As

the duke entered the Netherlands the Dutch nobles went out to meet him, hoping thus to gain his favor. But no favor was to be gained. "Welcome or not," said the duke, "it is all one. Here I am." The king had given him unlimited power and, indeed, he exercised it. He appointed a council of twelve members with a Spaniard at the head, and the people well named it the Council of Blood. He seized the property of the rich, he tortured the poor, and he had the beggars put to death. "The king," he declared, "would rather see the whole country a desert than allow a single heretic to live in it."

In the meantime Queen Elizabeth and the Protestant princes of Germany aided William of Orange, and he marched into the Netherlands at the head of an army. Two battles were fought, but William lost both. He then went to France, and soon raised a more powerful army of French, English, and German soldiers.

Philip recalled the Duke of Alva, and it was well that he did. On the first of April the beggars in the town of Briel raised the colors of the Prince of Orange, and the people sang on the street:

> "On April Fool's Day
> Duke Alva's spectacles were stolen away."

(The word briel in Dutch means spectacles.)

The king appointed a new governor who abolished the Council of Blood and pardoned the rebels. But this did not bring peace, and the war went on. The Spaniards were determined to conquer the town of Leyden (Li'den), but the Dutch were even more

SPAIN AND THE DUTCH

determined not to yield. For weeks the inhabitants had no bread or meat. Then a plague broke out and more than six thousand people died from disease and starvation. But the burgomaster of the town refused to surrender. "I have sworn to defend this city," he said, "and with God's help I mean to do it."

When hope seemed almost gone a carrier pigeon flew into the town with a message under its wing from the Prince of Orange. The message said that the dikes would be cut so that the sea could flood the land and wash the Spaniards from their fort. "Better a drowned land than a lost land," said the Dutch. And on the third of October, 1575, the dikes were cut, the Spaniards fled in terror as the sea flooded the land, and Leyden was saved. In memory of the heroic defense the Prince of Orange founded the University in the town. Not many years passed when the Pilgrims from England sought refuge in Holland and later sailed from Leyden to America bringing the love of liberty.

William the Silent

It was not long before the Dutch provinces united to expel the Spaniards and establish religious liberty; and this Union was the beginning of the Dutch Republic. The provinces chose William of Orange as their head, and he went to Delft to be inaugurated, but before the ceremony took place he was slain by an assassin. To this day the Prince of Orange is looked upon by the Dutch as the father of his country.

THE STORY OF SIR PHILIP SIDNEY

King Philip was indeed pleased when he heard of the death of William of Orange, for he had offered a large reward for the capture of the prince, dead or alive. The Spanish monarch still held the southern part of the Netherlands which we know to-day as Belgium. But the seven united provinces had thrown off his tyranny, and after the death of William, they elected his son to be president of their executive board. They then became known as the Dutch Republic, but to-day they are called the Kingdom of Holland. And the ruler of this kingdom is Queen Wilhelmina, a descendant of William of Orange.

After William's death there was more fighting between the Spaniards and the Dutch. Queen Elizabeth had secretly aided the Prince of Orange. Now she did not conceal her help, she sent English forces to the Netherlands. Several battles were fought, and at the siege of Zut'phen the queen's noblest courtier, Sir Philip Sidney, received a mortal wound. Bleeding and faint he was overcome with thirst, and he called for something to drink. After much difficulty a glass of water was brought to him, but as he was putting the cup to his lips he noticed the longing look of a wounded soldier near him. "Take it," he said, as he offered the water, "thy necessity is yet greater than mine." Soon after this the generous Sidney died. Among his last words were those to his brother, "Above all, govern your life by the will and word of your Creator."

All England grieved when Sir Philip Sidney died. His charming manner and his goodness of heart won the affection of the people, and his character to this day stands as a type of generous and noble manhood. Besides being a brave soldier he was a brilliant writer. In his story "Ar-ca'di-a" he wrote, "They are never alone that are accompanied with noble thoughts."

Shakespeare reading a play to Elizabeth

The century of Queen Elizabeth was indeed active in more ways than one. Besides Sir Philip Sidney the age produced many great writers. Edmund Spenser wrote his poem the "Faërie Queen" at this time. But above all stood William Shakespeare, the greatest of the world's dramatists.

THE INVINCIBLE ARMADA

Philip had indeed reasons to dislike England. She was not only a Protestant country, but she had seized his rich treasure ships as they were returning from America, and now she was helping the people of the Netherlands in their rebellion against him. "I will teach England a lesson," said the monarch whom all Europe feared, and it did not take him long to decide how he should do it.

The king of Spain was proud of his large war-ships. They could easily capture the small English vessels, he thought. He ordered the Spaniards to prepare a large fleet. This required a vast sum of money, and Spain was already heavily taxed because of her troubles with France and the Netherlands. But the king paid no attention to the burdens of the people. "We will conquer England for all time," he said, and more taxes were imposed upon Spain.

Philip toiled day and night sending messages and giving orders so that nothing would be forgotten and nothing overlooked. The Spaniards were truly busy, but none worked harder than the shipbuilders on the coasts.

A Spanish grandee

At last the ships were ready, and they looked like castles on the water. Philip called them the Invincible Armada — a fleet that could not be conquered. The Armada consisted of one hundred and thirty vessels, carrying more than twenty-five thousand men.

England was indeed frightened, and well she might be. But the people were determined that Philip should not invade their country, and their fleet consisted not only of royal war-ships, but even merchant vessels from small seaport towns were sent out. It is true their war-ships were smaller than the heavy slow-moving galleys of the Spaniards, and they were manned with fewer sailors. But they were quicker in movement and many of them were armed with newer guns.

Not only Protestants but Catholics fought for England. Her fleet was commanded by Admiral Howard, a Catholic; and under him was Sir Francis Drake, a Protestant.

It was in April, 1587, that Drake sailed out from Plymouth with a fleet of less than thirty ships. He was bound for the harbor of Ca'diz and there he would surprise the Spanish vessels defending the fort. He would singe King Philip's beard, he said. And, indeed, he did, for he soon entered the harbor and before his quick little ships sailed out, they had a store of provisions.

A year had passed since Drake sailed from Plymouth, and now the Invincible Armada set sail from Lisbon, Portugal, to conquer England. It drifted about the coast and it was three weeks reaching the English Channel. In July the two fleets faced each other off the coast of Cal'ais in France and soon the battle was begun.

The English had converted six of their vessels into fire-ships, and when these appeared in the darkness of the night sending forth their flames, the Spaniards were terrified. "Fire-ships! Fire-ships!" they cried. Then followed explosions. A panic seized the frightened crews and in their eagerness to escape they cut the cables, and the anchors went to the bottom of the sea. Those of the enemies' ships not disabled sailed to the north, for they did not dare to pass the English fleet that lay between them and Spain.

Terrible storms arose, and some of the Spanish ships were wrecked off the coast of Scotland, and only sixty-five battered vessels returned to Spain. Philip's fleet had failed, and England became mistress of the seas.

THE STORY OF GILBERT AND RALEIGH

Since the days of John Cabot, English fishermen had been going to the banks of Newfoundland for fish. But it was not till Queen Elizabeth's reign that England again turned her attention to America.

Raleigh's Servant finds him smoking

Explorers were still interested in a northwest passage to Asia. Martin Frob'-ish-er, an English seaman, had sailed to the coast of Labrador, and he had returned to England with the news that gold mines existed among the icebergs.

Later sailed one of the noblest of English seamen — Sir Humphrey Gilbert. But his small fleet was attacked by Spaniards, and then a terrible storm arose and Gilbert was compelled to return home. But the Queen did not lose faith in him; she gave him a little golden anchor, and fitted out other vessels for him. He soon set sail again, and this time, landing on the coast of Newfoundland, started to build a colony. But the long cold winters and the visits of warlike Indians did not make the place very attractive to the settlers. After exploring the coast Gilbert decided to return to England.

Again he encountered terrible storms, and the sailors had reasons to be frightened. But Gilbert said to them, "We are as near to heaven by sea as by land." And it was not long before his ship was lost in the stormy sea.

In his poem on Gilbert Longfellow tells us

> Alas, the land-wind failed,
>   And ice-cold grew the night;
> And nevermore, on sea or shore,
>   Should Sir Humphrey see the light.
>
> He sat upon the deck,
>   The Book was in his hand:
> "Do not fear! Heaven is as near,"
> He said, "by water as by land."

Walter Raleigh was Sir Humphrey Gilbert's half-brother. He, too, was eager to plant an English colony in America. Raleigh was one of the Queen's favorite courtiers, and she gladly gave him a charter to build a colony.

Not only did Elizabeth dress extravagantly, but her courtiers and the rich men of the time were clothed in brilliantly colored satins and velvets. And no one was more handsomely dressed than Sir Walter Raleigh. We remember that before he came to the court he placed his crimson velvet cloak over a muddy place in the road for the queen to step on.

Raleigh believed that his brother had gone too far north. He would plant his colony farther south; but first he would send out men to explore the land.

Accordingly two ships set sail, and they reached Roanoke Island off the coast of North Carolina.

It was in the summer when they landed, and they found sweet-scented flowers and an abundance of wild grapes. They explored the forests and there they noticed the pine, the cedar, and the cypress tree. They saw a great many birds and rabbits and deer, and they met friendly Indians. It is no wonder that the explorers returned to England with glowing accounts of the land that they had seen. "We will call this country Virginia in honor of our Virgin Queen," they said.

Jamestown in 1622

Other ships soon embarked from England. This time the men were not merely to explore but to plant a colony. They had no sooner landed than they began searching for gold, and colony planting seemed to be forgotten. The Indians told them to follow the Roanoke River to its source, and there they would find rich treasures.

They explored the river but found no gold mines,

and they returned to England without planting a colony. However, they took back with them plants unknown in Europe — the Indian corn, tobacco, and the potato. Sir Walter Raleigh and other Englishmen soon learned to smoke the tobacco. One morning, as Sir Walter was enjoying his pipe, a servant entered the room and, seeing his master enveloped in smoke, threw a tankard of ale over him.

Raleigh made another attempt to plant a colony. "This time," he said, "I will send families. The men will be more contented if they have home ties."

And it was not long before one hundred and fifty men, women, and children set sail for Roanoke Island. Their leader was John White, and he was to be their governor in the new country. Soon after landing a baby girl was born to Mrs. Dare, the daughter of Governor White. It was the first child born of English parents in America and it was named Virginia.

These settlers had landed in July, and now it was late in the fall. Food was becoming scarce and Governor White returned to England for supplies. He found great excitement in the home country. It was the year of the Spanish Armada, and every English vessel was forced into service. Three years passed before Governor White could set sail with the provisions for the little colony that he had left on Roanoke Island.

Now that the war on the waters between England and Spain was ended, Raleigh was free to fit out a vessel of supplies for his colony in America. It was agreed that if the people should leave the island, they would carve on the bark of a tree the name of the place to which they would go. If misfortune should overtake them, they would inscribe a cross on the tree.

Again Governor White set sail and reached the island. But there was no trace of the settlers except the word "Croatan" carved on the trunk of a tree. More than three hundred years have passed since then, and to this day we do not know what became of the Lost Colony and little Virginia Dare.

Raleigh's efforts, however, to plant a colony in America were not without fruits. He educated England into the idea of colonizing, and before many years had passed a permanent English colony was founded in America. And this was followed by other settlements. The time soon came when Spain lost part of her possessions in the new world, and it was left to the English colonies on the Atlantic coast to found a new nation. Thus the story of our country was begun.

SUGGESTIVE TOPICS FOR COMPOSITION AND DISCUSSION

The questions and suggestions that follow will be found of great value in familiarizing students with historic characters and events and in stimulating the imagination. The teacher should introduce other topics of a similar nature.

CHAPTER I

A day at Ellis Island.

Debate on the question, Resolved, That immigration should be restricted.

Are there any boys and girls in your school whose parents have come from foreign countries? If there are, what are the countries?

A comparison: the *Concord* with the Germans and an ocean greyhound with immigrants.

Imagine and describe a conversation between Pastorius and Penn.

The inventors of the alphabet.

John Gutenberg and the invention of printing.

The writing of manuscripts before printing was invented.

The picture writing of the Indians.

The sewing machine and its inventor.

The telephone and its inventor.

Make a list of recent inventions.

What do you know of their history?

CHAPTER II

How do geographic conditions affect a country?

How did the situation of Greece influence its civilization?

Read the myth of Apollo, the myth of Dionysus, and the myth of Demeter.

Read Hawthorne's "Wonder Book" and "Tanglewood Tales."

Read the story of the Odyssey. (The prose translation by George H. Palmer is excellent.)

The Marathon runner to-day. Read "Pheidippedes," a poem by Robert Browning.

Why I admire Leonidas.

What I admire in the character of Themistocles.

Has the United States a strong navy?

Why did the ancient people build walls around their cities?

Are there any pictures or statues in your school by Greek artists? If there are, who are the artists? Do you know the stories of the pictures or statues?

Are there any buildings in your city or town that look like Greek architecture? What are the characteristics of Greek columns?

A comparison: the Greek theater and the American.

What did the theaters do in ancient times that newspapers do to-day?

Is the object of the theater to-day to educate?

Are schools and colleges giving outdoor plays to-day?

Debate on the question, Resolved, That plays should be given in the schools.

What is done in dramatization in the different grades of your school?

Do modern educators believe that plays should be given in the schools?

A comparison: the education of a Greek boy and that of an American boy.

A comparison: the ancient Olympic Games and those of recent years.

Do you think the modern Olympic Games will promote a better feeling among nations?

CHAPTER III

Learn some of the fables of Æsop.

Modern Athens; its government.

With the help of the dictionary, make a list of words that have come down to us from the Greeks and note their meaning.

What would an American dislike in Solon's laws? What was good in them?

A comparison: a modern court of justice and the Areopagus.

What is meant by the expression "rich as Crœsus"? Do you know any other persons whose names stand for types?

What is the meaning of the word "tyrant" to-day?

What do you think of the changes in Solon's constitution by Clisthenes?

The oracle at Delphi.

What I admire in the character of Socrates.

What I admire in the boyhood of Alexander the Great.

What modern city do you think is the world's intellectual and commercial center to-day?

In what was Claudius Ptolemæus ahead of his time?

What were the Seven Wonders of the World?

What America owes the Greeks.

CHAPTER IV

Read Macaulay's "Horatius at the Bridge."

What I admire in the character of Horatius.

Why was George Washington called the "Cincinnatus of the West"?

Did Washington ever pursue a "Fabian" policy?

With the help of the dictionary make a list of words that have come from the Romans and note their meaning.

The Roman Forum.

Hannibal, the Carthaginian commander.

What I admire in the characters of the Gracchi.

CHAPTER V

Who besides Cicero has been called the "Father of his Country"?

The character of Julius Cæsar as a general.

What I admire in the character of Vercingetorix.

What did Cæsar accomplish for the welfare of his country?

Read what Cassius and Brutus say of Cæsar in Shakespeare's play "Julius Cæsar." Is the character of Cæsar as portrayed by Shakespeare in accord with that of history?

Learn part of Mark Antony's speech (Shakespeare's "Julius Cæsar") beginning "Friends, Romans, countrymen."

How does Mark Antony describe Brutus at the close of Shakespeare's play?

Read Plutarch's "Lives of Great Men."

Who was the first ruler to be called emperor? What rulers of modern times are called emperors? Why are they given the title?

The Roman Colosseum.

A comparison: the Greeks and the Romans.

What America owes the Romans.

Read the story of Christ from the Bible.

CHAPTER VI

Why do the French remember Clovis?

Read the story of King Arthur from Tennyson's "Idyls of the King," or from Malory's "Morte d'Arthur," or from Sidney Lanier's "Boys' King Arthur."

APPENDIX

What is the meaning of the term "Vikings"?

Read the Anglo-Saxon story of Beowulf. (See "Siegfried and Beowulf," by Madame Ragozin.)

Read the story of Siegfried, the hero of the North, from William Morris' "Sigurd the Volsung."

Read a description of the Normans and Saxons from "Ivanhoe," by Sir Walter Scott.

Why I admire Alfred the Great.

The Great Charter.

The origin of the English Parliament.

A comparison: English Parliament and United States Congress.

The origin of the title "Prince of Wales." When the eldest son of the English ruler is invested as Prince of Wales, where does the ceremony take place? Describe the ceremony.

The Stone of Scone.

What I can learn from Robert Bruce. Read "Bannockburn," a poem by Robert Burns.

The meaning of the expression "Middle Ages."

Have we any organizations in modern life that take the place of the old gilds?

What was there good in knighthood?

On whom is the title of knighthood conferred in Great Britain to-day? Describe the ceremony?

Are there any organizations in the United States whose members are called knights?

Read the description of a tournament in "Ivanhoe," by Sir Walter Scott.

Read "The Tournament," a poem by Sidney Lanier.

What are the duties of the Archbishop of Canterbury in the coronation of an English monarch?

A comparison: a Greek temple and a cathedral of the Middle Ages.

What we owe the monasteries of the Middle Ages.

CHAPTER VII

The Koran.

The Mohammedans to-day.

What we owe to the crusades.

Modern Jerusalem.

Read Scott's "Ivanhoe" in order to study the times of King Richard.

Read "Robin Hood," by Howard Pyle (describing the outlaws in King Richard's time).

The Children's Crusade.

· The early Italian painters; the stories of their lives and pictures.

A comparison: the oldest university in England and the oldest university in our country.

CHAPTER VIII

Read the "Norse Stories Retold," by Hamilton Mabie.

Read the "Story of Vinland," a poem by Sidney Lanier.

Read the "Norsemen," a poem by John Greenleaf Whittier.

Read the "Saga of King Olaf," from Longfellow's "Tales of a Wayside Inn."

Read Longfellow's "Skeleton in Armor."

Read "The Norseman's Ride," a poem by Bayard Taylor.

Read "Norseland Tales," by H. H. Boyesen.

Read "Jan of Iceland," by Bayard Taylor, from his "Boys of Other Countries."

What was China called in Marco Polo's day?

Read Coleridge's poem "Kubla Khan."

Does America owe anything to Marco Polo?

The ideas in regard to Asia in the fifteenth century.

What did Bartholomew Diaz accomplish?

APPENDIX

How did the trade with the East lead to the discovery of America?

How did the capture of Constantinople by the Turks bring about the discovery of America?

Did Columbus owe anything to the crusades?

Read the story of the "Alhambra," by Washington Irving.

Read "Columbus at the Convent," a poem by John T. Trowbridge.

Read "The Thanksgiving for America," a poem by Hezekiah Butterworth.

Read "Columbus," a poem by Edward Everett Hale.

Read "Columbus and the Mayflower," a poem by Lord Houghton.

What I admire most in the character of Columbus.

Read Joaquin Miller's poem "Columbus."

Do you think America ought to have been named after Columbus?

Debate on the question, Resolved, That Columbus Day should be observed by our country.

How did Portugal vie with Spain?

Who found the first ocean route to India?

What great voyage helped to prove that the earth is round?

How did the search for riches lead to the discovery of a great ocean?

What I admire most in the character of Magellan.

Was France interested in a route to China?

Modern Mexico.

How did the search for gold lead to the discovery of a great river?

CHAPTER IX

What countries in Europe to-day have state churches?

What is the meaning of Protestant?

What household comforts and conveniences have come into use since the times of Queen Elizabeth?

Read "Kenilworth," by Sir Walter Scott.

Why I admire Lord de Bayard.

Read "Brave Little Holland," by Griffis.

Read "Hans Brinker," by Mary Mapes Dodge.

The city of Delft is noted for what earthenware?

Queen Wilhelmina.

What I admire in William of Orange.

Why I admire Sir Philip Sidney.

Read Lamb's "Tales from Shakespeare."

Why did Spain lose her stronghold in America?

Which country is more powerful to-day — Spain or England? Reasons for your answer.

Read Longfellow's poem, "Sir Humphrey Gilbert."

Read "Raleigh's Cell in the Tower," a poem by Dante Gabriel Rossetti.

How did England come to be the founder of our country?

A BIBLIOGRAPHY
AND HOW TO USE IT

BY ALISON J. BAIGRIE

BRANCH LIBRARIAN, CHATHAM SQUARE BRANCH, NEW YORK PUBLIC LIBRARY

HISTORY is a subject in which no real work can be done by the use of one book and only one. A collection of books illustrating and enlarging each phase of the subject should be readily accessible, either in the class-room itself or in the public library. In almost every town will be found a public library ready and willing to bring the schools into closer touch with the materials available there for study, and the accompanying list is designed as a working aid to teachers and pupils. The material included can all be found in any good library and has had the test of practical use.

There are many ways of interesting children in following up a subject which is a part of their daily work. Much of this must be done in the class-room, but the following plan has been tried in New York and found to be successful. The class visits the library, accompanied by the teacher, and a talk, sometimes in story form, is given which illustrates or emphasizes a subject to be brought out in the class-room. This may be an incident in the life of a great man, or an historic legend, or any similar topic. At the same time the librarian has ready a collection of books containing related or similar incidents or stories, and at the close of the talk the children are given an opportunity to look at the books, and encouraged to take them out on their library cards. When the teacher wishes this to be done, a sufficient number of books for use by the class as a whole is obtained, and the books are used for supplementary reading. In many cases this plan has led to the reading of most of the books upon a given subject by the children, and teachers have remarked upon the added intelligence and interest in the class-room work.

If it is not possible for the class to visit the library in a body, the work can be done through the teacher and the individual pupil, and the time and effort spent will be amply justified by results. In many of the New York schools, class visits to the branch libraries are a regular part of the school work.

In order that the children may make the most of this sort of teaching, it would be advisable to have them receive instruction in the use of reference books and the card catalogue. This may be given during other class visits to the library. The talk on reference books should be simple and clear, free from technicalities, and may include the general make-up of a book, stating what the title page is and the difference between an index and a table of contents. The question of arrangement follows, and the dictionary may be used as an illustration. Then the kinds of encyclopædias are briefly described, and a standard work in each class explained. For instance, the "New International" is a good example of a general encyclopædia, and the Champlin's Young Folks' Cyclopædia may be shown as illustrating how special reference books take up one or two subjects only. The gazetteer, the almanacs, and the Harper's Encyclopædia make up a list which is sufficient for any except more advanced classes. After the explanations are finished it is a good plan to ask actual reference questions, allowing the children to find the answers, and thus testing the knowledge acquired. The alert intelligence of the replies received shows that the interest of the children has not only been aroused, but held. This oral review should be followed by a written report in school where the subject of the class work is made a topic of composition.

The talk on the use of the catalogue should also be very simple, and the explanations made very clear as to its use. The only difficult question is that of subject headings, but this can be handled from the standpoint of the grade of the children. When the talk is finished, have the children find books on given subjects by referring to the catalogue. This work may be made the subject of a second report if the teacher wishes, or the two can be combined into one. As a result of this work, other plans for broadening the work in history will suggest themselves to the teachers, and also other ways of using the same plans.

The following lists have been arranged according to the chapter divisions of this book, since this method has seemed to be the one most likely to be useful to teachers using the book as a textbook, and the lists for pupils and teachers have been separated for the same reason. The list for teachers includes those books which have proved most useful in the experience gained in public library work, and the children's list is made up of titles which are of definite value and interest. It includes all that could be well used by the child doing the regular grade work in history, and much of it could be used for class-room work by teachers as story material and supplementary reading.

A few titles have been included which cannot be called history, and this has been done because of the conviction that such books are valuable as aids both to teachers and pupils in grasping the spirit of an age or epoch, or a phase in development. "The Promised Land," for instance, is not history, but the teacher who reads it will teach the subject of emigration with a fuller understanding and a deeper sympathy. The reaching out into the by-paths of a subject is of intense value, and it is hoped that the lists will be found useful for this purpose.

CHAPTER I

TEACHERS

ANTIN. — Promised land
CLODD. — Story of the alphabet
FISKE. — Discovery of America
HART. — American history told by contemporaries. Vol. 1
HILDRETH. — United States. Vol. 2
HOLLAND. — Historic inventions
SCHAUFFLER. — Scum of the earth

PUPILS

EGGLESTON. — Our first century
GORDY. — American explorers
GUERBER. — Story of the thirteen colonies
ELSON AND MACMULLAN. — The story of our country

CHAPTER II

TEACHERS

BROWNING, R. — Echetlos
BURROWS. — Discoveries in Crete
BURY. — History of Greece
FERGUSON. — Hellenistic Athens
GULICK. — Life of the ancient Greeks
GOODSPEED. — History of the ancient world. Rev. ed.
HERODOTUS. — History; tr. by Rawlinson, ed. by Grant
HOLM. — History of Greece. Vol. 1

JEBB. — Greek literature
MAHAFFY. — Old Greek life
MOREY. — Outlines of Greek history
MYERS. — Ancient history
PLUTARCH. — Lives; tr. by Dryden, ed. by Clough

PUPILS

BROOKS. — Story of the Odyssey
CHURCH. — Pictures from Greek life and story
KINGSLEY. — Heroes
WESTON. — Plutarch's lives for boys and girls
WHITE. — Our young folks' Plutarch

CHAPTER III

TEACHERS

ABBOTT. — Pericles
CAPPS. — From Homer to Theocritus
FAIRBANKS. — Mythology of Greece and Rome
GRANT. — Greece in the age of Pericles
GUERBER. — Myths of Greece and Rome
HOLM. — History of Greece. Vol. 2
MAHAFFY. — Social life in Greece
MOREY. — Outlines of Greek history
SHUCKBURGH. — History of the Greeks
WHEELER. — Alexander the Great
ZIMMERN. — Greek history

PUPILS

ARNOLD. — Stories of ancient peoples
BALDWIN. — Old Greek stories
BURT. — Stories from Plato
CHURCH. — Lords of the world

CHURCH. — Three Greek children
GUERBER. — Story of the Greeks
HAAREN AND POLAND. — Famous men of Greece

CHAPTERS IV-V

TEACHERS

ABBOTT. — Roman political institutions
BOTSFORD. — Story of Rome
BOTSFORD. — Roman assemblies
DILL. — Roman society from Nero to Marcus Aurelius
DILL. — Roman society in the last century of the Roman emperors
FERRERO. — Women of the Cæsars
FOWLER. — Julius Cæsar
GIBBON. — Students' history of Rome
GOODSPEED. — History of the ancient world. Rev. ed.
GOODYEAR. — Roman and mediæval art
HOW AND LEIGH. — History of the Romans to the death of Cæsar
LAING. — Masterpieces of Latin literature
MORRIS. — Hannibal
PLUTARCH. — Lives; tr. by Dryden, ed. by Clough
SEIGNOBOS. — History of the Roman people
THOMAS. — Roman life under the Cæsars

PUPILS

ANDREWS. — Ten boys
CHURCH. — Pictures from Roman life and story
CLARKE. — Story of Æneas
COUCH. — Historical tales from Shakespeare
GUERBER. — Stories from Shakespeare's historical plays
GUERBER. — Story of the Romans

HAAREN AND POLAND. — Famous men of Rome
LAING. — Heroes of the seven hills
LAMB. — Tales from Shakespeare
MORRIS. — Historical tales — Roman
WESTON. — Plutarch's lives
WHITE. — Our young folks' Plutarch

CHAPTER VI

TEACHERS

ADAMS. — Civilization during the Middle Ages
ASSER. — Life of King Alfred
CHURCH. — Beginnings of the Middle Ages
EMERTON. — Introduction to the Middle Ages
FREEMAN. — William the Conqueror
GREEN. — Short history of the English people
HENDERSON. — History of Germany
HILL. — Liberty documents. Vol. 2
KEARY. — Vikings in West Christendom
MACY. — English constitution
MALORY. — Morte d'Arthur
MUNRO. — History of the Middle Ages
THATCHER AND SCHWILL. — General history of Europe

PUPILS

BALDWIN. — Story of Roland
BLAISDELL. — Stories from English history
BROOKS. — Historic boys
GRIERSON. — Children's book of English minsters
HAAREN AND POLAND. — Famous men of the Middle Ages
LANG. — Book of romance
MARSHALL. — Island story
MACLEOD. — Book of King Arthur and his noble knights

PYLE. — King Arthur and his knights
SEYMOUR. — Chaucer's stories
STONE. — History of England
TAPPAN. — When knights were bold
TAPPAN. — Heroes of the Middle Ages
YONGE. — Book of golden deeds

CHAPTER VII

TEACHERS

ARCHER AND KINGSFORD. — Crusades
BROWN. — Venetian republic
Chronicles of the Crusades
CHURCH. — Crusaders
ROBINSON. — History of western Europe
THATCHER AND SCHWILL. — General history of Europe

PUPILS

BLAISDELL. — Stories from English history
BUXTON. — Stories of the Crusades
DOUGLAS. — Heroes of the Crusades
GUERBER. — Story of the English
PYLE. — Men of iron
YONGE. — Prince and the page
ZOLLINGER. — Rout of the foreigner

CHAPTER VIII

TEACHERS

CHANNING. — History of the United States
FISKE. — Discovery of America
HART. — American history told by contemporaries.   Vol. 1
JOHNSON. — Pioneer Spaniards in North America

LAWLER. — Columbus and Magellan
OLD SOUTH LEAFLETS. — No. 20, Coronado; Nos. 29, 31, Columbus; Nos. 37, 115, Cabots
OLSON. — The Northmen, Columbus and the Cabots
PARKMAN. — Pioneers of France in the New World
PRESCOTT. — Conquest of Mexico
THWAITES. — France in America
WINTERBURN. — The Spanish in the Southwest

PUPILS

COXHEAD. — Mexico
GORDY. — American explorers
GORDY. — American beginners in Europe
GRIFFIS. — Romance of discovery
HALE. — Stories of discovery
HIGGINSON. — Young folks' book of American explorers
McMURRY. — Pioneers of the Mississippi Valley and the West
McMURRY. — Pioneers on land and sea
SHAW. — Discoverers and explorers
ELSON AND MACMULLAN. — The story of our country

CHAPTER IX

TEACHERS

CREIGHTON. — Sir Walter Raleigh
FROUDE. — English seamen in the sixteenth century
HILDRETH. — United States. Chaps. I–II
HUME. — Philip II
LEE. — Great Englishmen of the sixteenth century
MOTLEY. — Dutch republic
PAYNE. — Hakluyt; Voyages of Elizabethan seamen
PARKMAN. — Pioneers of France in the New World

PUPILS

ANDREWES. — Story of Bayard
GRIFFIS. — Brave little Holland
JENKS. — Book of famous sieges
KELLY. — Story of Sir Walter Raleigh
MORRIS. — Historical tales — English
WRIGHT. — Children's stories in English literature

INDEX

A Becket, Thomas, 146
Achilles, 23-24
Acropolis, 37, 42
Ægean Sea, 17
Æneas, 67
Æneid, 67
Æquians, 74
Æschylus, 41
Æsop, 52, 53
Agamemnon, 23
Alba Longa, 74
Alcibiades, 56
Alemanni, 117
Alesia, 96
Alexander the Great, 58-66
Alexandria, 65
Alexius, 152
Alfred, King, 123-130
Alhambra, 173
Alva, Duke of, 213
Americans, 1-5, 130
Americus Vespucius, 177
Angles, 115
Anio, the, 73
Aphrodite, 20, 21, 22, 40
Apollo, 19, 25
Arabs, 148
Archons, 50-51
Areopagus, 52, 54, 57
Ares, 20
Ariovistus, 92-93
Aristophanes, 56
Aristotle, 58, 61

Armada, Invincible, 217
Artemis, 19
Arthur, King, 118-121
Ascalon, 157
Ashdown, 127
Assassins, 157
Assyria, 14
Athene, 19, 21, 22, 25, 38
Athenian education, 42
Athens, 28, 31, 34-46, 49-58
Augustine, 121
Augustus, Cæsar, 103-104
Aurora, 19, 20
Aztecs, 192

Babylon, 64
Badon Hill, 119
Bannockburn, battle, 139
Balboa, 182-184
Barbarossa, 154
"Beggars," 213
Bible, the, 14
Blondel, 159
Britain, 119
Britons, 12, 119
Bruce, Robert, 139
Brutus, 102-103

Cabot, John, 178-180
Cabot, Sebastian, 178
Cælian Hill, 69
Cæsar, Caius Julius, 87-103
Caius Gracchus, 84-86

INDEX

Cambridge, University of, 162
Campus Martius, 106–107
Cannæ, 80
Canterbury Cathedral, 146
"Canterbury Tales," 147
Cape of Good Hope, 171
Capitol, the, 105
Capitoline, the, 104
Carolina, Fort, 208
Carthage, 76–82, 112
Cartier, Jacques, 187–191
Cassius, 102
Catiline, 90–91
Cato, 81, 89
Ceres, 20
Chaucer, Geoffrey, 147
Christ, 109, 148
Christianity, 107–112
Cicero, M. Tullius, 87, 89, 95
Cicero, Quintus, 95
Cid, the, 173–174
Cimabue, 163
Cincinnatus, 74–76
Claudius Ptolemæus, 66
Cleopatra, 100
Clisthenes 53
Clotilda, 116–118
"Clouds, The," 56
Clovis, 116–118
Codrus, 49
Coligny, Admiral, 208
Colosseum, 107
Columbus, Bartholomew, 172
Columbus, Christopher, 66, 172–178
Compass, mariner's, 13
"Concord," the, 7–8
Constantine, Emperor, 111
Constantinople, 111

Cornelia, mother of Gracchi, 84, 86
Cortez, Hernando, 191–195
Crassus, 89, 98
Crito, 57
Crœsus, 28, 52
Crusades, 148–164
Cynics, the, 62

Da Gama, Vasco, 180–182
Danes, the, 1, 122–128
Dante, 162
Darius, 28–31
De Bayard, Lord, 206
Delaware River, 6, 7, 8
Delft, 215
Delphi, 31, 50, 55
Demeter, 20
Demosthenes, 58–59
De Soto, Ferdinand, 197–199
Diana, 19
Diaz, Bartholomew, 171–172
Diaz, Porfirio, 195
Diogenes, 62
Dionysus, 41
Discus Thrower, the, 40, 43
Dorians, 49
Draco, 51
Drake, Sir Francis, 202–206
Duke of Alva, 213
Duke Leopold, 157
Dutch, the, 6, 211, 216

Edward I, of England, 137
Egbert, King, 122
Egypt, 64, 100, 112
Egyptians, 15
El Dorado, 197, 199
Electricity, 13
Elizabeth, Queen, 202, 217

Ellis Island, 3
England, 12, 119
Eos, 19
Eric the Red, 166
Ericson, Leif, 6, 166–167
Esquiline Hill, 105
Ethelred, 124
Ethelwulf, 123
Etruria, 70, 112
Etruscans, 70, 106
Eucles, 30
Euripides, 41
Europeans, 3

Fabius, 79–80
Ferdinand, King, 176
Fort Carolina, 208
Forum, the, 73, 86, 105
France, 12
Francis I, King, 206
Franks, the, 12, 115–118
Frederick I, Emperor, 154
Frobisher, Martin, 220

Gaul, 89
Gauls, the, 12, 91–97
Genoa, 162
Germans, the, 5–10, 92–93
Germantown, Pa., 9–10
Gilbert, Sir Humphrey, 220
Gild-halls, 143
Gilds of London, 143
Giotto, 163
Godfrey of Bouillon, 152
"Golden Hind," 204
Good Hope, Cape of, 171
Gordian knot, the, 63
Goths, 115
Gracchi, the, 84–86
Gracchus, Caius, 84–86

Gracchus, Tiberius, 84
Granada, 173
Great Charter, 134
Greece, 17, 18, 28
Greeks, the, 16, 17–66, 107, 108
Gregory, Pope, 121
Gutenberg, John, 14, 16
Guthrum, 128

Hades, 20
Hannibal, 78–81
Harold, King, 131–132
Hastings, battle of, 131–132
Hawkins, John, 201–202
Hector, 23–24
Helen of Troy, 21, 22
Hellespont, 32
Helvetians, the, 92
Hengist, 119
Henry III, King, 135–137
Hephæstus, 20, 24
Heptarchy, 122
Hera, 19, 21, 41, 52
Hercules, 47–48
Hermes, 19, 40, 41
Herodotus, 48
Hestia, 20
Hieroglyphics, 15
Holland, 211
Homer, 14, 21, 27, 43, 53, 61
Horace, 113
Horatius, 69–72
Horsa, 119
House of Commons, 136
House of Lords, 137
Howard, Admiral, 219
Huguenots, 209
Hyphasis, the, 64

246 INDEX

Iliad, the, 20, 27, 43, 61
Immortals, the, 33
Inca, 197
Indians, 11, 15
Isabella, Queen, 176
Italians, 12

Jamestown, Va., 5, 6
Jerusalem, 149
John, King, 132–134
Juan Perez, 175
Juno, 19
Jupiter, 19, 67
Jutes, 115

Koran, the, 148
Knighthood, 144–145
Kublai Khan, 168–170

Ladrones, 186
Langton, Stephen, 133
Lake Geneva, 92
Laocoon, 25
Lars, Porsenna, 70
Latins, the, 67
Lavinia, 67
Leisler, Jacob, 6
Leonidas, 31–34
Leopold, Duke, 157
Leyden, 214
Louvre, 40
Lyceum, 42, 53
Lydia, 27

Macaulay, Lord, 71
Macedonia, 58
Magellan, Ferdinand, 184–187

Magna Charta, 134
Marathon, battle of, 27–31
Marathon race, 48
Marathon runner, the, 30
Marco Polo, 168
Mardonius, 35
Marius, 88
Mars, 20
Mayflower, the, 5
Mecca, 149
Medina, 149
Melos, 40
Menelaus, 21, 22
Menendez, 210
Mercury, 19
Mexico, 191
Middle Ages, the, 139–147
Milan, 206
Miltiades, 29–30
Minerva, 19
Minuit, Peter, 6
Mississippi, 199
Mohammed, 148–149
Mohammedans, 148
Montezuma, 192
Montfort, Simon de, 136
Montreal, 190
Moors, the, 173
Müller, Waldsee, 6
Museum, 41
Myron, 40

Naples, 206
Natal, 182
Neptune, 20
Nero, 110
Netherlands, The, 211
Nicolo Polo, 168
Normans, the, 130–132
Northmen, the, 122, 165–168

INDEX

Octavius Cæsar, 103–104
Odoacer, 116
Odysseus, 25
Odyssey, 20, 27, 43
Olaf, King, 166
Olympic games, 46–48
Olympus, 19
Ovid, 113
Oxford, University of, 162

Pacific Ocean, 184
Palatine Hill, 69, 105
Panama, 183, 195
Paris, 22
Paris, France, 118
Parliament, English, 135, 137, 139
Parthenon, 39–41
Parthians, 98
Pastorius, Daniel, 8–10
Patroclus, 23
Paul, 109
Paula, 111
Pedagogue, 42
Penn, William, 5–9
Pennsylvania, 6–9
Perez, Juan, 175
Pericles, 38–42
Persia, 28, 58, 64
Persians, the, 36
Peru, 196–197
Peter the Hermit, 150
Petrarch, 163
Pharos, 66
Pharsalus, 100
Phidias, 39–40
Philadelphia, 9
Philip II of France, 154
Philip of Macedon, 58
Philip II of Spain, 211

"Philippics, The," 58
Phœnicians, the, 16
Pindar, 48
Pisistratus, 43, 53
Pizarro, 195–197
Platæa, 36
Plato, 58
Pluto, 20
Polo, Marco, 168
Polo, Nicolo, 168
Pompey, 88, 98–100
Pontius Pilate, 109
Pontus, 101
Pope Gregory, 121
Port Royal, S. C., 6
Portugal, 172, 200
Porus, 64
Poseidon, 20
Praxiteles, 40
Priam, 22
Printing, 13–16, 26
Ptolemy, 65–66, 100
Punic Wars, 76–82

Quakers, the, 8, 10
Quebec, 190
Quirinal Hill, 69

Raleigh, Walter, 221
Regulus, 77
Remus, 68–69
Richard I, King, 132, 154–159
Rio de la Plata, 185
Roanoke Island, 222
Romans, 12, 16
Rome, 11, 67–86
Romulus, 68–69, 105
Rubicon, 98–100
Runnymede, 134

Sabines, the, 69, 105
Sacred Mount, 72–73
St. Augustine, 210
Saladin, 154 St. Paul, 109
Salamis, 34–35
Sardinia, 76
Saxons, the, 115
Scandinavians, the, 1
Scipio, 81–84
Scots, the, 138–139
Senlac Hill, 131
Sewing machine, the, 13
Shakespeare, William, 217
Sicily, 76
Sidney, Sir Philip, 216
Simon de Montfort, 136
Slavery, 10
Socrates, 54–58
Solon, 43, 51–53
Sophists, the, 54
Sophocles, 41
Spain, 100, 200
Sparta, 21, 22, 29, 32, 37, 44–46
Spenser, Edmund, 217
Stone of Scone, the, 138
Styx, 24
Sulla, 88
Swedes, the, 1, 6

Tacitus, 115
Tarquin, 69–70
Themistocles, 31–34, 37
Thermopylæ, 32–34
Theseum, 41
Theseus, 49
Tiber, the, 67
Tiberius Gracchus, 84–86
Tower of London, 143
Trasimene, Lake, 78

Trebia, 78
Tribunes, 73
Troy, Siege of, 20–27, 67
Turks, 39, 150
Tyrker, 6

Ulysses, 25
Urban, Pope, 149–151

Valencia, 173
Varro, 80
Vasco da Gama, 180–182
Vatican, 40
"Veni, vidi, vici," 101
Venice, 161–162, 180
Venus, 20, 40, 67
Vercingetorix, 95–97
Vesta, 20, 106
Vestal Virgins, 106
Vikings, the, 121–123
Villeins, 141
Vinland, 167
Virgil, 67
Virginia, 5
Virginia Dare, 223
Vulcan, 20
Vulgate, 111

Wilhelmina, Queen, 216
William the Conqueror, 131–132
Welsh, the, 138

Xantippe, 55
Xerxes, 31–35

Yucatan, 191

Zana, 81
Zeus, 19, 21, 47
Zutphen, 216

CPSIA information can be obtained
at www.ICGtesting.com
Printed in the USA
BVHW091141260421
605876BV00013B/204